ASIAN HISTORICAL DICTIONARIES
Edited by Jon Woronoff

1. *Vietnam,* by William J. Duiker. 1989
2. *Bangladesh,* by Craig Baxter and Syedur Rahman. 1989
3. *Pakistan,* by Shahid Javed Burki. 1991
4. *Jordan,* by Peter Gubser. 1991

Historical Dictionary

of the

Hashemite Kingdom of

JORDAN

by
PETER GUBSER

Asian Historical Dictionaries, No. 4

The Scarecrow Press, Inc.
Metuchen, N.J., & London
1991

British Library Cataloguing-in-Publication data available

Library of Congress Cataloging-in-Publication Data

Gubser, Peter.
    Historical dictionary of the Hashemite Kingdom of Jordan /
Peter Gubser.
      p. cm. — (Asian historical dictionaries ; no. 4)
    ISBN 0-8108-2449-3
    1. Jordan—History—Dictionaries. I. Title. II. Series.
DS154.G83   1991
956.9504'3'03—dc20
                                   91-25171

For Annie

and

Sasha and Christi

CONTENTS

Editor's Foreword   vii

A Note to the Reader   ix

Abbreviations and Acronyms   xi

Chronology   xiii

INTRODUCTION   1

THE DICTIONARY   15

BIBLIOGRAPHY   89

EDITOR'S FOREWORD

Jordan, as the author of this book rightly stresses, is at the crossroads of Middle Eastern events. It is involved in the Palestinian issue, relations with Israel, currents in the broader Arab and Islamic worlds, and international relations with the great powers. But, as he also shows, it has always been at the crossroads, long before the present kingdom was established and, due to its geographic position, it will continue to be involved in and affected by broader movements in this sensitive and turbulent area.

There is, however, much more to Jordan than what appears in the media when one event or another catches the public's eye. Domestic politics are no less lively; relations among various ethnic, religious, and social groups must be adjusted; the economy has to develop to meet the needs of an expanding population; and cultural and educational progress cannot be neglected. So this dictionary looks both inward and outward to inform anyone interested in discovering how Jordan has managed to fare as well as it has under exceptionally trying circumstances. The reader may be a student or scholar, diplomat, businessperson, or first-time visitor to an intriguing place.

We are pleased that this historical dictionary of Jordan has been written in a very straightforward and accessible manner by someone who knows the country well. Peter Gubser, who is now president of American Near East Refugee Aid (ANERA), has traveled widely and written extensively on Jordan, where he has done considerable field research. His writings include *Jordan: Crossroads of Middle Eastern Events*, whose theme was referred to above.

Jon Woronoff
Series Editor

A NOTE TO THE READER

The spelling of Arabic words can be problematic, so I have chosen a pragmatic and contemporary approach. If a name is well known to the international public, I accept that spelling rather than a strict transliteration (e.g., Nasser, not Nasir). If most contemporary books spell a place name in one way while older ones in another, I accept the contemporary usage (e.g., Karak, not Kerak). Otherwise, I use standard transliteration with minimal diacritical marks, according to Hans Wehr's *Dictionary of Modern Written Arabic* (5th ed. New York: French & European Publications, 1985).

Peter Gubser
President
ANERA
Washington, D. C.
June 1991

ABBREVIATIONS AND ACRONYMS

ACC	Arab Cooperation Council
FATAH	Movement for the Liberation of Palestine (reverse acronym for the Arabic)
GNP	Gross National Product
JAA	Jordan Arab Army
JCO	Jordan Cooperative Organization
JDP	Jordan Development Plan
JVA	Jordan Valley Authority
LAS	League of Arab States
NCC	National Consultative Council
NPC	National Planning Council
PFLP	Popular Front for the Liberation of Palestine
PLO	Palestine Liberation Organization
PNC	Palestine National Council
RSS	Royal Scientific Society
TFF	Transjordanian Frontier Force
UAK	United Arab Kingdom
UAR	United Arab Republic
UNRWA	United Nations Relief and Works Agency (for Palestine Refugees)

CHRONOLOGY

pre-10,000 B.C.	Paleolithic Age.
10,000–4500 B.C.	Mesolithic Age.
6000 B.C.	Human habitation known in region.
4500–3000 B.C.	Chalcolithic Age.
3000–1200 B.C.	Bronze Age.
2400 B.C.	Advanced sedentary agricultural civilization flourished in region.
1200–300 B.C.	Iron Age. Region settled by four Semitic groups.
ca. 950 B.C.	Israelites conquer region.
854 B.C.	Assyrians invade region.
850 B.C.	King Mesha of Moab gains control of region.
ca. 580 B.C.	Babylonians invade region.
ca. 500 B.C.	Nabatean Arab tribe establishes presence in region.
330 B.C.	Alexander the Great of Greece conquers region.
312 B.C.	Ptolemaic rule commences.

ca. 70–60 B.C.	Romans gain control of region.
ca. A.D. 200	Ghassanid Arab tribe establishes presence in region.
ca. A.D. 330	Region converts to Christianity under Roman Emperor Constantine.
A.D. 629–636	Arab Muslims conquer region.
A.D. 661–750	Umayyads rule region from Damascus.
A.D. 750–1071	Abbasids rule region from Baghdad.
1071	Seljuk Turk rule from Baghdad established.
ca. 1100	European Crusaders conquer region.
1187	Crusaders defeated at Karak and leave Jordan.
1187	Saladin (Salah al-Din) reestablishes Arab Muslim rule under Ayyubid dynasty.
1260	Mamluk rule established in the region.
1518	Ottomans conquer region.
ca. 1600	Ottoman direct control of region wanes.
1831	Egyptian ruler Muhammad Ali conquers region.
1841	Ottomans regain control.
1880–1890	Ottomans establish direct rule in region.

1900–1908   Hejaz-to-Constantinople railroad built
                through Jordan.

1914   World War I starts.

1917–1918   Jordan conquered by Sharif Hussein's
                forces and the British.

1919   Amir (Prince) Faisal, son of Sharif
                Hussein, rules Jordan from Damascus.

1920   Faisal declared king; Britain given
                mandate over Jordan (then called
                Transjordan) and Palestine at San
                Remo Conference; Faisal driven out of
                Damascus by French forces; British
                high commissioner for Palestine
                declares Jordan to be a British
                mandate; Amir Abdullah, another son
                of Sharif Hussein, enters Jordan.

1921   Amir Abdullah meets Colonial Secretary
                Churchill and is accepted as the ruler
                of Jordan under the British mandate.

1922   The Arab Legion, Jordan's armed forces,
                founded; Colonel F. Peake is first
                commander.

1922   Saudi Arabia unsuccessfully invades
                Jordan.

1924   Saudi Arabia again unsuccessfully invades
                Jordan.

1928   Jordan's Organic Law (constitution)
                promulgated; Anglo-Jordanian Treaty
                signed; first Legislative Council elected.

1930	Major John Glubb assigned by Britain to the Arab Legion.
1932	Bedouin raiding stopped by Glubb's unit of the Arab Legion.
1941	Arab Legion helps Britain suppress pro-Axis coup in Iraq.
1946	A new Anglo-Jordanian Treaty signed; Abdullah declared king of the Hashemite Kingdom of Jordan; new constitution promulgated.
1948	Anglo-Jordanian Treaty of 1946 renegotiated; Israel declares independence; Jordan occupies West Bank of the Jordan.
1948–1949	First Arab-Israeli war.
1949	Jordan signs armistice with Israel.
1950	Parliamentary elections held on both the East and West Banks of the Jordan; parliament declares both banks of the Jordan united as the Hashemite Kingdom of Jordan.
1951	King Abdullah assassinated; his son, Talal, crowned king.
1952	King Talal removed from office due to illness; his minor son, Hussein, declared king, but regency council rules.
1953	King Hussein takes oath of office and assumes duties of the crown.

1954	Johnston Plan to divide Jordan River waters proposed.
1954	Parliamentary elections.
1955	Jordan pressured to join Baghdad Pact; riots throughout country.
1956	General John Glubb dismissed from Arab Legion command
1956	Arab-Israeli war; Jordan does not participate.
1956	Parliamentary elections.
1956–1958	The United States replaces Britain as Jordan's major patron.
1957	King Hussein foils major coup attempt.
1958	British troops temporarily sent to Jordan as Lebanon experiences civil war.
1961	Parliamentary elections.
1962	Parliamentary elections.
1964	Arab Summit creates Palestine Liberation Organization, decides to divert headwaters of the Jordan River, and establishes United Arab Command; in Jerusalem, the first Palestine National Council meeting is held.
1966	Jordan bans the Palestine Liberation Organization.

1967	Parliamentary elections; subsequent national parliamentary elections delayed until 1989.
1967	Arab-Israeli war; Jordan loses the West Bank to Israeli military occupation; United Nations Security Council Resolution 242 issued.
1970	Jordan fights the Palestine Liberation Organization factions in Jordan; Syria briefly invades Jordan.
1971	Jordanian prime minister assassinated by Palestinian faction.
1972	King Hussein proposes that the East Bank and West Bank be federated in a United Arab Kingdom.
1973	Jordan participates in 1973 Arab-Israeli war, but on Syrian soil.
1974	Rabat summit of Arab heads of state declares the Palestine Liberation Organization to be the sole legitimate representative of the Palestinian people.
1974	King Hussein dissolves parliament.
1975	Start of decade-long period of rapid economic growth.
1976	Parliament recalled to suspend elections, then dismissed anew.

1976	Jordan and Syria sign broad cooperation agreements.
1978	King Hussein appoints a National Consultative Council as a partial and temporary replacement for parliament.
1978	Camp David Accords signed; Baghdad summit of Arab heads of state promises significant funding for confrontation states, including Jordan.
1980	Jordan supports Iraq in war with Iran.
1980	Summit of Arab heads of state held in Amman.
1981	Jordanian-Syrian border tensions.
1983	King Hussein dismisses National Consultative Council.
1984	Parliament is recalled; by-elections held in East Bank.
1984	Palestine National Council meets in Amman.
1985	King Hussein and Palestine Liberation Organization Chairman Yasser Arafat agree on a framework for peace.
1985	Decade long period of strong economic growth ends.
1986	By-elections held in the East Bank.
1987	Hussein-Arafat framework suspended.

1987	Special summit of Arab heads of state held in Amman.
1988	Jordan withdraws politically and administratively from the West Bank.
1988	Jordan, Egypt, Iraq, and North Yemen form the Arab Cooperative Council.
1989	Riots in provincial capitals; popular demands for political and economic reforms and an end to corruption.
1989	Parliamentary elections, noted for openness and freedom, held in November.
1990	In April, King Hussein appoints a royal commission consisting of 60 members from throughout Jordanian society and all political trends to write a national charter outlining the rules for political life in the country.
1990	In August, Iraq invades and occupies Kuwait.
1990	From August through December, 900,000 third country nationals flee to Jordan from Kuwait. Jordan, in massive effort with international aid, assists the evacuees in their repatriation.
1990	Approximately 240,000 Jordanians (mostly of Palestinian origin) leave Kuwait and take up residence in Jordan.

1990	The Persian Gulf crisis, inspired by the Iraqi invasion of Kuwait, provokes broad and passionate political debates in Jordan and the Middle East; in practice, the Arab Cooperation Council is suspended; the Persian Gulf conflict and attendant U.N. sanctions cause a severe economic crisis in Jordan.
1990	In December, the royal commission completes and endorses the National Charter on Jordanian political life.
1991	In January-February, by means of a major war, the coalition partners force Iraq out of Kuwait; Jordan does not participate in the war or join the U.S.-led coalition.
1991	The United States includes Jordan in another major attempt to resolve the Arab/Palestinian-Israeli conflict.
1991	In June a national conference of 2,000 leaders endorses the National Charter and it is signed by the king.

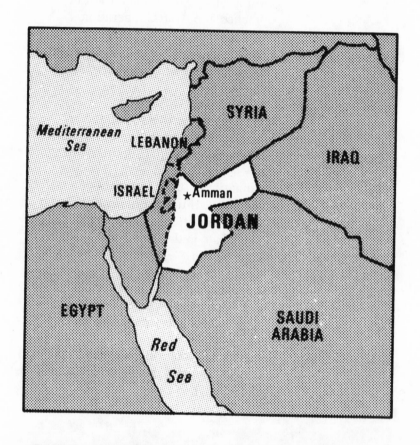

Official Name: Hashemite Kingdom of Jordan

INTRODUCTION

OVERVIEW

Jordan lies in the heart of the Middle East. It is bordered on the north by Syria, on the east by Iraq, on the south by Saudi Arabia, and the west by Israel and the West Bank. Aqaba, at the southern-most tip of Jordan, is its only outlet to the sea. Its 35,000 square miles (90,649 square kilometers) are marked by deserts, mountains, deep valleys, and rolling plains. An area of low rainfall, it is mostly desert; only 3% is arable (partly under irrigation), and 1% is forested.

Jordan's rapidly growing population reached approximately 3,600,000 (based on the 1979 census) in 1991. About 55% of the population have their roots in Jordan, the balance are of Palestinian origin. Ethnically, though, the people are overwhelmingly of Arab stock. With respect to religion, the vast majority of the population is Sunni Muslim. Approximately 5% are Christian, Druze, or Shia Muslim. Less than a fifth of the population is economically active. Services, agriculture, light industry, mining, trade, and construction are the sectors that employ most of the work force. Jordan is poor in terms of natural resources. It does extract some phosphate and potash, but does not have the petroleum production enjoyed by some of its Middle East neighbors. In many ways, its educated population is its main resource, both for local economic activity and as an export to its oil-rich neighbors. Despite the influx of numerous Palestinian refugees and a very rudimentary economic base, starting in the late 1940s Jordan's essentially free-market economy has grown steadily with notable downturns, especially during periods of internal strife or war.

Jordan as a distinct geographical or political entity did not exist throughout most of recorded history, but its land is central in the Middle East, a crossroads for the many waves of history that have swept across the region. During ancient times, empires such as the Assyrians, Egyptians, Israelites, Greeks, and Romans conquered and ruled the region. In the early seventh century the Arab Muslims established their control. Their various dynasties ruled the area, with a hundred-year break during the Christian Crusader conquest, until they were defeated by the Ottomans in 1518.

Jordan, then known as Transjordan, came into existence as a British mandate following the breakup of the Ottoman Empire at the end of World War I. The first ruler of Jordan, Amir (Prince) Abdullah of the Hashemite family from Mecca, oversaw the establishment of the government (a constitutional monarchy) and the extension of its control over present-day Jordan. In 1948 at the birth of Israel and as a product of the first Arab-Israeli war, Jordan occupied the West Bank of the Jordan River. This territory, through a parliamentary procedure, was annexed to the kingdom in 1950, but was lost to Israel in the Arab-Israeli war of June 1967. The West Bank and its population, primarily Palestinian Arabs, remains under Israeli military control in 1991, but is considered a disputed territory. King Hussein acceded to the Hashemite throne in Amman in 1953, making him one of the longest-ruling heads of state in the world.

GEOGRAPHY AND CLIMATE

Jordan's geography is marked by three distinct systems. The most striking feature is the Jordan River Valley. At 1,296 feet below sea level, it is the lowest point on earth. The valley receives very little rain, but since the 1960s the Jordanians have developed a sophisticated irrigation system in the valley so that it can be intensively cultivated. Because it is warm in the winter, off-season fruits and vegetables can be produced. The Transjordan Plateau runs like a wedge from the Syrian border to slightly below the Dead Sea at Ma'an. It consists of broad, rolling plains, occasionally cut by precipitous valleys called wadis. Rain-fed agriculture is practiced here. To the south and east of the plateau lies the Arabian, or Syrian, Desert, a vast wasteland only sparsely populated by bedouin.

Jordan is not rich in natural resources. Its only commercially viable minerals are potash and phosphates. Jordan has no known oil deposits. Its important rivers are the Yarmuk (shared with Syria), the Jordan (shared with Israel and the West Bank), and the Zarqa. Except for the small oasis of Azraq in the eastern desert, Jordan has no natural lakes. An artificial lake rises behind the Talal Dam on the Zarqa River.

Jordan enjoys a warm, pleasant climate, but with limited rainfall over most of the country. In the winter in the capital, Amman, the average high and low temperatures are 52°F and 40°F; in the summer they are 86°F and 64°F. In the northern part of the Transjordan Plateau, rainfall averages 25 inches, but in the southern part it falls to an erratic 12 to 14 inches, barely sufficient to raise a wheat crop. The desert and the Jordan Valley receive up to 10 inches of rain. Typical of the eastern Mediterranean, the rain falls only during the winter and early spring.

JORDAN'S PEOPLE

Jordan's 3.6 million people are concentrated in the more fertile highlands, a narrow strip paralleling the West Bank and Israel from the Syrian border to the southern end of the Dead Sea. The majority, about 55%, are Jordanians who originate from the land east of the Jordan River. Most of the balance have their origins in Palestine. They came to Jordan as refugees following the 1948 and 1967 Arab-Israeli wars. Others moved to Amman during the period when the West Bank was part of Jordan. While relations between the two groups are relatively peaceful today, Palestinian elements did conduct an unsuccessful civil war against the Jordan government in 1970 and 1971. Both groups are of Arab stock and consider themselves to be part of the larger Arab nation. About 5% of Jordan's population are members of the Arab Christian minority. They enjoy positive relations with the Muslim majority and hold high positions in commerce and government. Ethnic minorities are even smaller; they consist of Armenian Christians and Circassian Muslims. The latter group, wearing their traditional uniforms, are royal palace guards.

Arabic is the official language of Jordan. The written language is virtually the same throughout the Arab world. The spoken language in Jordan falls within the general dialect of eastern Mediterranean Arabic. In Jordan, there are slight variations in the spoken language between the rural and urban areas and between the Palestinians and Jordanians. The influence of television, radio, and education have caused many of these differences to moderate or disappear. The ethnic minority groups, while they speak Arabic in public, often retain their mother tongue at home. English is widely taught and spoken. Many government documents are published simultaneously in Arabic and English, and there is an English channel on television.

Jordan is a highly urban country. About 70% of the people live in towns of 5,000 or more. About 1,000,000 live in Amman, the capital. Twenty years ago, there was stark contrast between urban and rural standards, the former enjoying many more basic amenities, such as running water, electricity, and government services. Today those differences have largely but not entirely disappeared. In towns, 99% of the homes have electricity; in the villages the figure is 81%. The data for running water is 92% and 78% respectively. Due to the artificial influx of the Palestinian refugees and the very high birth rate, Jordan is highly overpopulated given the resources of its land. Currently, 60% of the population are below 20 years of age—a heavy burden on the economy and service sector. While the urban areas, consisting of many small apartment buildings and houses, certainly have some crowded quarters, they do not approach the poor conditions often associated with Third World countries. About 10% of the population live in Palestinian refugee camps where the housing is the most congested. In the rural area, about

25% live in stone and mud houses, while less than 5% follow the traditional life of the Arab bedouin, living in tents and tending camels and sheep. The bedouin retain much of their ancient dress, characterized by their flowing robes and silver-clad daggers. In the villages and urban areas, traditional dress is giving way to European-style clothes, although the men still frequently wear the head cloth called a *kufiya*.

Jordan is officially a Muslim country. Ninety-five percent of the people adhere to that faith and almost all are Sunni, or orthodox, Muslims as opposed to Shia Muslims. The government supports the established religion through its Ministry of Awqaf and Islamic Affairs. Islam deeply affects the lives of many Jordanians. Praying five times a day, attendance at mosque for Friday prayers, fasting during the month of Ramadan, tithing, and the pilgrimage to Mecca are aspired to and practiced by many. In addition, the wave of Islamic fervor that has affected the Middle East for the last two decades has not bypassed Jordan. Some practice their religion more assiduously and publicly. Religious classes and discussions at mosques are in demand and some women dress in modern but modest long coats and head scarves.

Greek Orthodoxy is the religion of most of the Christians, but various other eastern and western rites are found as well. These groups follow their age-old rituals, often in the language of their religious forefathers: Greek, Armenian, and Syriac.

JORDAN'S HISTORY

The first known inhabitants of the land of Jordan date back to 6000 B.C. Their presence is indicated through various monuments and drawings, such as in the ancient city of Jericho. Around 2000 B.C., during the Bronze Age, the area first appears in recorded history. Four Semitic peoples—Edomites, Moabites, Ammonites, and Amorites—lived in the area from south to north. Their economy was based on agriculture and trade. They were variously conquered by the Hittites, Egyptians, Assyrians, Babylonians, and Persians. While these conquerors left little imprint on Jordan, such others as the Israelites, Greeks, and Romans did. In the tenth century B.C., the great Israelite kings David and Solomon subjugated and ruled the region, but under King Mesha in 850, the Moabites regained control and extended their rule throughout most of the land of Jordan. The Nabateans, an Arab-speaking people, gained control in about 500 B.C. Famous for trade, they ruled from their unique capital carved out of the rose-colored stone cliffs of Petra. The Nabateans were present when the Greeks, led by Alexander the Great, conquered the territory. Subsequently their architecture and arts strongly reflected the presence of the Greeks and their successors, the Seleucids and the Ptolemies, the latter of whom ruled from Egypt. By 70 B.C. the Romans extended their empire over Jordan. Eventually they were to build vast trading cities at the present-day locations of Amman, then Philadelphia, and Jerash where extensive, well-preserved ruins still exist. Under its successor, the Byzantine Empire, the region was converted to Christianity under the great Emperor Constantine (A.D. 324–337). The locally dominant Arab tribe, the Ghassanids, who had displaced the Nabateans, also converted to Christianity. Due to internal decay and frequent warfare with the Persian Empire, Byzantine rule seriously declined.

Between 629 and 636 Arab Muslims coming from Arabia conquered the Fertile Crescent. The first battle with the Byzantines was at Mu'ta near present-day Karak where the Muslims suffered defeat. At Yarmuk, just north of Jordan in Syria, the Muslim Arabs were successful and thereafter established their control and religion in the region. Jordan was ruled by a succession of Muslim dynasties: the Umayyads of Damascus, the Abbasids of Baghdad, and the Fatamids of Egypt. During this period, Jordan was a backwater in terms of economics and trade. The pilgrimage route to Mecca, though, did pass through the region, and Umayyad leaders built summer palaces there.

In the late eleventh century, parts of Jordan, Palestine, and Lebanon fell to the Christian Crusaders from Europe. Historically and religiously, the region was central to both Christianity and Islam. For the former, Christ lived and taught around

Jerusalem. For Islam, Jerusalem is one of its three holy cities, the site of the Prophet Muhammad's ascension to heaven on his faithful steed Buraq. In Jordan, the Crusader Renard de Châtillon ruled from Karak in ancient Moab, where he built a magnificent fortress that still stands. In 1099 the Crusaders conquered Jerusalem, but in 1187 they were defeated by the Muslim leader Saladin (Salah al-Din), who established the Ayyubid dynasty. One consequence of the Crusader era was that many local Arab Christians converted to Islam. Also, in some localities, blond hair and blue eyes are not uncommon because of intermarriage and the taking of many European slaves.

Having gained control of Asia Minor and southern Europe by the end of the fifteenth century, the Ottoman Turks turned their attention to their fellow Muslims in the Arab world. In 1518 they easily defeated the Mamluks and incorporated most of the region in their empire. While exerting considerable direct control in more populated regions, such as Syria and Palestine, the Ottoman Empire ruled the land of Jordan indirectly, if at all. In the early nineteenth century, the Egyptians under Muhammad Ali briefly held sway over the eastern Mediterranean, including Jordan. Only in the late nineteenth century did the Ottomans reassert direct control. During this period, they brought Circassian tribesmen to settle in the area of Sweileh and Amman. Throughout the Ottoman period, the people of Jordan were nomadic herdsmen and peasant tillers of the soil. The only element of importance to outsiders was that the route to Mecca still passed through the region. The Ottoman rulers maintained relations with the local bedouin tribes, often through payments but occasionally via military excursions, in order to sustain the security of this route. From 1900 to 1908 the Hejaz railroad linking Asia Minor to the area surrounding Mecca was built through Jordan. This new mode of transport marginally raised the importance of the area, but contributed significantly to its economy.

During World War I, Transjordan (as it was then called) was the scene of most of the fighting of the great Arab Revolt against Ottoman rule. Assisted by the British and the famous Lawrence of Arabia (T. E. Lawrence), Sharif Hussein of Mecca led this successful revolt, which contributed to the Ottoman defeat in World War I and to the eventual establishment of the various Arab states. Jordan originally fell under the rule of King Faisal, son of Sharif Hussein and the principal military leader of the Arab Revolt. Jordanians, along with their Arab brothers from other regions, served in the new Arab government and sat in its parliament. After King Faisal was forced from the throne in July 1920 by the French military, the British high commissioner of Palestine, Sir Herbert Samuel, went to the town of Salt in Transjordan and declared that the territory, as had been secretly agreed by the British and French in the Sykes-Picot Agreement during World War I, was part of the British mandate of Palestine. Amir (Prince) Abdullah, a younger son of Sharif Hussein, arrived in Jordan in the fall of 1920 with the intent of regaining Damascus for his Hashemite family. Because he had gained a following, the British decided to recognize his leadership in that territory and provide him with a subsidy in exchange for his not pursuing his original Damascus intentions. This arrangement was confirmed in a March 27, 1921, meeting between then colonial secretary, Winston Churchill, and Amir Abdullah. In addition, Jordan was officially removed from Britain's Palestine mandate and given a mandate status of its own.

Between the two world wars, Amir Abdullah, with considerable assistance from Britain, established Hashemite authority in Jordan, basing his rule in the new capital of Amman. Security was established through the creation of the Arab Legion, first led by Colonel Frederick Peake and later by General John Bagot Glubb, both British officers. The apparatus of a state—a government with its normal functions and a parliament—was established. Abdullah's ambitions to extend Hashemite control over more Arab areas did not abate, but were not realized until after World War II. In 1928 the Anglo-Jordanian Treaty was signed, ostensibly giving Jordan its independence. The reality was that true independence, duly recognized by other nations, was not realized until the late 1940s.

In many ways, Jordan's importance in the world is defined by its neighbors to the west: Israel and the Palestinians. During World War I, Britain issued the Balfour Declaration, which stated that the British government viewed with favor "the establishment in Palestine of a national home for the Jewish people." In addition, the civil and religious rights of the existing non-Jewish communities (the Palestinians) would not be prejudiced. In the ensuing years, thousands of Jewish immigrants arrived, primarily from Europe. This influx resulted in conflict between the Jews and the local Palestinian Arab population that the British mandatory rulers could barely contain. Amir Abdullah and Jordan, though neighbors, were largely removed from these developments until the creation of the State of Israel.

The Hashemite Kingdom of Jordan came into being as a result of the March 1946 and March 1948 Anglo-Jordanian treaties. It gained a much greater degree of freedom than it had enjoyed in the 1928 treaty, and the mandate was officially ended, though the British retained considerable influence over the regime. Soon after these important developments, Jordan took part in the first Arab-Israeli war (1948–1949). At its termination, Jordan occupied the West Bank, but was saddled with a large refugee population. Basically, Jordan's population was tripled from a prewar 400,000 by the addition of 400,000 Palestinians who were resident in the West Bank and 450,000 Palestinian refugees from Israel. In 1950 a newly elected parliament, made up of an equal number of members from the West Bank and the East Bank of the Jordan, voted to join the two territories as the Hashemite Kingdom of Jordan. On the one hand, the addition of the Palestinians was a depressant to the Jordanian economy because of the services the refugees required. On the other, some Palestinians brought expertise, entrepreneurship, and savings that stimulated the economy. The presence of the two Palestinian groups also created new political tensions as West Bank residents vied for power with the East Jordanians who then dominated the system. This political competition folded into the broader regional struggle then focused on moderate and radical interpretations of Arab nationalism.

In 1951 King Abdullah was assassinated by Palestinian elements disgruntled by his secret negotiations with Israeli leaders. He was succeeded by his son, Talal. In a constitutional move, Talal was removed from the throne in 1952 due to mental illness. He was succeeded by his son, Hussein. Being a minor, King Hussein did not take up his duties until he reached the age of 18 by the Muslim lunar calendar (about 17½ by the Gregorian calendar) in May 1953.

During the 1950s, due to internal and external influences arising from the competition among Arab states, the strong emotions around the concept of Arab nationalism, and the conflict between the United States and the Soviet Union, Jordan was decidedly unstable. In this troubled time, the Arab Legion, which was renamed the Jordan Arab Army and commanded by a Jordanian Arab from 1956, was crucial to the survival of the Hashemite throne. Also, Jordan's principal Western supporter shifted from Britain to the United States in the late 1950s.

The 1967 Arab-Israeli war was disastrous for Jordan. Its causes were first, severe disagreement between the Arabs and Israelis over how the waters (rivers and lakes) of the Jordan Valley should be divided among the riparian states; second, the continuing Palestinian refugee problem, which in 1964 resulted in the creation by the League of Arab States (then led by Egypt's Gamal Abdel Nasser) of the Palestine Liberation Organization (PLO), which was to challenge Israel; third, the creation of a unified Arab military command for the states neighboring Israel; and fourth, numerous harsh Israeli raids into Arab territory, often in response to forays by Palestinian refugees. As a consequence of the Arabs' decisive defeat in the June 1967 war, Jordan lost the West Bank, Egypt the Sinai, and Syria the Golan Heights to Israeli military occupation.

In Jordan, Palestine guerrilla presence grew substantially in the 1968–1970 period. By the summer of 1970, the guerrillas formed a virtual second government, a severe challenge to the Jordanian authorities, that degenerated into a civil war by

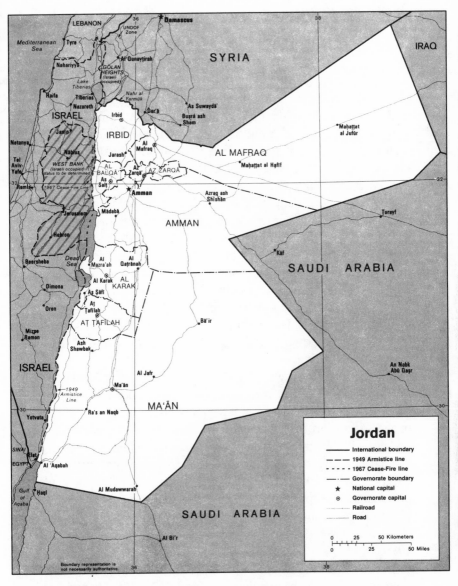

September. Despite the additional intervention of Syria on the side of the Palestinian forces, King Hussein (with indirect help from the United States and Israel) prevailed within a month, but mopping-up action lasted into 1971. Once again the Jordan Arab Army was central to the survival of the Hashemite monarchy.

Jordan played a minimal role in the next Arab-Israeli war, in 1973. It committed only a few troops who fought on Syrian soil against the Israeli army. Jordan did not benefit from the war as did Egypt and Syria. Israel partially pulled back from the Sinai and the Golan Heights, but not from the West Bank. In 1974 King Hussein was dealt a diplomatic blow at the meeting of Arab heads of state in Rabat, Morocco. This important summit declared that the PLO was the sole legitimate representative of the Palestinian people, undermining the king's claim to the West Bank and his standing with some of his own Palestinian citizens. Despite this move, Jordan kept open the Jordan River bridges so that West Bankers, who were still Jordanian citizens, could travel freely back and forth to the East Bank for family, education, and business purposes. Additionally, Jordan continued to pay the salaries of its civil servants still resident in the West Bank. Jordan's only benefit from the 1973 Arab-Israeli war was economic. The country and many of its citizens were able to tap the newly found oil wealth in neighboring Middle Eastern countries.

The decade starting in 1974 witnessed rapid social and economic development in Jordan. It was a boom period for business, government development projects, growth in services, and broad expansion of the country's infrastructure. This change was not matched by commensurate political progress. There was no parliament and no elections, but development progress dampened somewhat the pressures arising from this lack of political life. Responding to the public's desire for more participation in governmental decision making, the king recalled parliament in 1984 and by-elections were held in that year and in 1986.

In the 1980s Jordan's relations with the PLO fluctuated from severe strain to close coordination. On July 31, 1988, in a major move, King Hussein dissolved parliament, which had been elected from the West and East Banks in 1967, and officially declared Jordan's political and administrative disengagement from the West Bank. This decision followed a major break with the PLO in 1986 and the onset in 1987 of the sustained Palestinian uprising (*intifada*) against the Israeli military occupation in the West Bank and Gaza Strip whereby the local Palestinian population clearly demonstrated its loyalty to the PLO. Aside from recognizing a political reality, the king's actions focused the world's attention on the necessity of solving the Israeli-Palestinian problem between the two parties themselves, not just as a minor part of the Arab-Israeli conflict. Also, during the following two years, Jordanian-PLO relations shifted from acute competition to at least partial harmony.

The 1989–1991 period was a true watershed for domestic politics in Jordan. For a few days in spring 1989, East Jordanians in provincial capitals rioted. Their demands were an end to economic reforms stipulated by the International Monetary Fund, ousting of corrupt politicians, restoration of press freedoms, and parliamentary elections. During the ensuing months, the regime responded on all fronts except economic reforms (new taxes, fewer subsidies), which were retained. Most importantly, the press regained its freedom, political meetings were allowed, and free and open parliamentary elections—the first on a nationwide basis since 1967—were held in November. To establish the parameters of Jordanian political life, in April 1990 the king appointed a royal commission of 60 noted people to write a national charter. In December, the commission completed and endorsed the charter, which stresses democracy and pluralism and allows for the formation of Jordanian-based and -financed political parties. In June 1991, a national conference of 2,000 leaders endorsed the National Charter and the king signed it.

Regionally, Jordan usually enjoyed strong relations with most of the moderate Arab states. In the Iran-Iraq war, Jordan sided with Iraq, lending it port facilities in Aqaba and sending volunteer troops. In 1988 King Hussein was a leader in establishing the Arab Cooperation Council (ACC), which joined Egypt, Iraq, Jordan, and North Yemen for purposes of political and economic cooperation. This relatively normal course of events was shattered when Iraq invaded and occupied Kuwait in August 1990. While Jordan strongly condemned the invasion, it also questioned the introduction of non-Arab, non-Muslim troops into Saudi Arabia. Favoring a negotiated solution and no war, Jordan did not join the United States-led coalition to oppose Iraq and its actions. From another perspective, as a consequence of the Persian Gulf crisis, from August through December, 900,000 third country nationals, largely Egyptians and South Asians, fled to Jordan from Kuwait and, to a lesser extent, Iraq. Jordan, in a massive effort with international aid, assisted the evacuees in their repatriation. In addition, approximately 240,000 Jordanians, mostly of Palestinian origin, left Kuwait and took up residence in Jordan. Another consequence of the conflict and the attendant United Nations sanctions was a severe economic downturn in Jordan that continued into 1991. Lastly, the ACC for all practical purposes became moribund.

Aside from the major Persian Gulf crisis, on the international scene, Jordan remained decidedly pro-Western. King Hussein's relations with the United States were occasionally strained, though, over differences on how the Arab-Israeli and Palestinian-Israeli problems should be addressed. However, in pursuit of the elusive peace, during the spring and summer of 1991, the U.S. was undertaking another attempt to resolve this long-standing conflict and Jordan was once again central to the diplomatic process.

THE DICTIONARY

ABBASIDS. The Abbasids ruled the Muslim Arab world, including Jordan, from Baghdad from A.D. 750 until they were displaced by the Muslim Seljuk Turks in 1071.

ABDULLAH IBN HUSSEIN, KING. Abdullah, son of Sharif Hussein ibn Ali (q.v.) of Mecca, was born in that Hejaz city, the most holy city in Islam, in 1880. A strong political adviser to his father, he urged Sharif Hussein to initiate the great Arab Revolt against the Ottoman Empire during World War I. After his brother, King Faisal (q.v.), was driven out of Damascus by French forces in the summer of 1920, Amir (Prince) Abdullah arrived in Jordan with an entourage of followers in the fall of that year. In 1921 then British Colonial Secretary Winston Churchill accepted him as the ruler of Jordan, but under the British mandate. In the early years, Amir Abdullah, with the cooperation of the mandatory power, Great Britain (q.v.), established the basic institutions of the state: a government, parliament (Council of Notables, later replaced by the Legislative Council), a constitution (the Organic Law), and the military (the Arab Legion) (q.v.). In 1946 an Anglo-Jordanian treaty (q.v.) was signed, to be revised in 1948. The amirate, or princedom, became the Hashemite Kingdom of Jordan, and Abdullah was crowned king. In 1948 King Abdullah's Arab Legion entered the Arab-Israeli war and occupied the West Bank (q.v.). By this action, King Abdullah partially realized his dream of ruling over a larger Arab state: following parliamentary elections on the East and West banks of the Jordan, the two banks were united as the

15

Hashemite Kingdom of Jordan in 1950. On July 20, 1951, angered by Jordan's secret negotiations with Israel (q.v.), a Palestinian assassinated King Abdullah in Jerusalem's most holy shrine, Haram al-Sharif. King Abdullah had two sons, Talal (q.v.) and Nayif. *See also* INTRODUCTION: JORDAN'S HISTORY, HASHEMITES, KING HUSSEIN.

ABU NUWAR, ALI (1924–   ). General Ali Abu Nuwar, a protégé of the young King Hussein (q.v.), was made the first Arab commander of the Jordan Arab Army (q.v.) in 1956. He, however, in collusion with other well-positioned Arab nationalists, led a military cabal in 1957 that attempted to overthrow the king and Hashemite rule. The king personally put down the attempted coup, saved Ali Abu Nuwar from physical harm by the loyal troops, and then exiled him.

AGRICULTURE. Jordan's landmass is dominated by desert; only 3% of its surface is cultivated. The main products of the irrigated Jordan Valley (q.v.), the agriculturally most productive area of Jordan, are vegetables and citrus, part of which is exported. In the highlands, fruit trees and grains are cultivated. Jordan is only 50% self-sufficient in wheat production, however. In the marginal areas next to the desert, the bedouin (q.v.) and peasants (fellahs) (q.v.) practice animal husbandry, raising primarily sheep and goats. The bedouin occasionally still raise camels, but this practice has declined greatly with the advent of the truck as the primary vehicle for overland trade. Chicken factories and sheep feedlots were introduced in the 1970s, primarily in the highland areas. Land is broadly distributed among the farming population, most farms being small or medium size: 75% of holdings (almost 75% of the land) is farmed by owners. Cultivation practices are increasingly modern, especially in the highly developed Jordan Valley. This modernization has contributed to the decline—50% in the last 15 years—in farm labor as a proportion of the total labor force.

ALEXANDER THE GREAT (356–323 B.C.). Alexander the Great of Macedonia brought the Jordanian region into direct contact with European culture for the first time, an interrelationship that would endure until this day. His reign was short (330–323 B.C.), but he initiated a prosperous period for the region during which Hellenic culture was encouraged, cities were built, and Jordan became a crossroads for the trade routes of the area.

ALLON PLAN. The Allon Plan, named for Israeli Foreign Minister Yigal Allon, appeared in the early 1970s. Its purpose was to reorder relations between Jordan and Israel with respect to the West Bank (q.v.), which Jordan had lost to Israel in the 1967 Arab-Israeli war. The plan proposed that Israel would return to Jordan most of the population and about 70% of the land of the West Bank. Israel would retain possession of and a military presence in the balance of the land, including a strip along the Jordan River. The plan was not acceptable to the Jordanian government and was never implemented. See also ARAB-ISRAELI CONFLICT, ISRAEL.

AMIR. In Arabic, the word amir means prince. Most sources refer to Abdullah ibn Hussein (q.v.) as an amir before he came to Jordan and in the period prior to 1946 when he became king of the Hashemite Kingdom of Jordan. In the literature in English, his sons and grandsons are usually referred to as princes (before they became kings, as did Talal ibn Abdullah [q.v.] and Hussein ibn Talal [q.v.]).

AMIRATE OF TRANSJORDAN. Prior to becoming the Hashemite Kingdom of Jordan in 1946, Jordan was officially the Amirate of Transjordan. An amirate is a princedom. See also AMIR.

AMMAN. Amman, the capital of Jordan, has a population of about one million. Unlike the ancient capitals of other Arab countries, Amman is a new town. Before 1875 Amman was the site of the long-forgotten biblical town of Rabbath Ammon and, later, the once prosperous Roman city of Philadelphia. Indeed, Roman ruins may still be found in Amman. Circassians (q.v.) encouraged by the rulers of the Ottoman empire (q.v.) settled in the area in the 1880s. Over the years, their village developed a minor reputation as a transport and trade center. This economic activity was greatly enhanced by the construction of the Hejaz Railroad (q.v.) just three miles east of the village in 1905. In 1921, Amir Abdullah established his capital in Amman. Despite this administrative role, the town's population had reached only a modest 20,000 by the mid-1940s. Subsequent to the influx of Palestinians (q.v.) starting in 1948, however, growth was extremely rapid: 108,000 in 1952; 648,587 in 1979; and over 1,000,000 in 1991. This growth may be ascribed to the rural-to-urban migration as well as to the arrival of many Palestinian refugees.

ANGLO-JORDANIAN TREATIES. The British and the Jordanians have signed three treaties. The first was in 1928, the second in 1946, and the third in 1948. The first treaty ostensibly gave Jordan its independence, but in reality this was a sham. Great Britain (q.v.) retained considerable military, fiscal, and political rights in the country, which was not compatible with any true definition of independence. The second treaty marked the end of the Amirate of Transjordan and the emergence of the Hashemite Kingdom of Jordan. Amir Abdullah (q.v.) officially became king following the signing of the treaty. Great Britain still retained some military and political rights in the country, and Jordan's independence was not widely recognized in the world. The third treaty curtailed still further British rights in Jordan and set the country on the road to actual independence. *See also* INTRODUCTION: JORDAN'S HISTORY.

AQABA. Aqaba is Jordan's only port. Located at the northern end of the Gulf of Aqaba and at the southern end of the country, Aqaba's economy is dominated by port activities, tourism, and some industry recently established along the coast.

ARAB COOPERATION COUNCIL (ACC). Formed in 1988, the Arab Cooperation Council is made up of Egypt (q.v.), Iraq (q.v.), Jordan, and North Yemen. These countries joined together to cooperate politically and economically for their mutual benefit. Due to the Persian Gulf Crisis and War (q.v.), the ACC became moribund.

ARAB-ISRAELI CONFLICT. The essence of the Arab-Israeli dispute revolves around two peoples' claims over the same land: the land of Palestine (q.v.), or that land which lies between the Jordan River (q.v.) and the Mediterranean Sea. The two peoples are the Jews and the Arab Palestinians (q.v.). The conflict arose during the last hundred years as Zionist Jews sought to settle in Palestine and eventually established the State of Israel (q.v.) in part of the land of Palestine. In reaction, the Palestinians, and the Arabs more broadly defined, objected politically and eventually militarily. The Arab-Israeli conflict has degenerated into war on five occasions: 1948–1949, 1956, 1967, 1973, and 1982. Jordan participated in the first, third, and fourth of these wars. Many efforts have been made to resolve the conflict. To date, only one has been partially successful, namely, the Camp David Accords (q.v.), which resulted in the 1979 peace treaty between Egypt and Israel. *See also* INTRODUCTION: JORDAN'S HISTORY, WARS, WEST BANK.

ARAB LEAGUE. *See* LEAGUE OF ARAB STATES

ARAB LEGION. An Arab reserve force, Jordan's original embryonic army, was founded in 1921 with British assistance.

In 1923 it was reorganized and named the Arab Legion. Its first commander was Major F. G. Peake (q.v.). It helped establish the authority of the state in the early years of Amir Abdullah's rule and along with the British air force drove back Saudi incursions in 1922 and 1924. Major J. B. Glubb (q.v.) joined the Arab Legion in 1930. Under his leadership, it started recruiting bedouin, making them into very loyal supporters of the Hashemite state. The Arab Legion participated in the 1948–1949 Arab-Israeli war during which it occupied the West Bank. In 1956 the British commander of the Arab Legion, then General Glubb, was relieved of his duties and the force was renamed the Jordan Arab Army. *See also* JORDAN ARAB ARMY.

ARAB NATIONALISM. The concept of Arab nationalism revolves around the feeling of unity—whether it be cultural, social, political, economic, or other—in the Arab world. Having led the great Arab Revolt against the Ottoman Empire, the Hashemites (q.v.) have substantial claim to being the most important initiators and sustainers of Arab nationalism. On the continuum of radical to conservative, Jordan is usually placed closer to the latter in its interpretation of Arab nationalism. King Hussein's (q.v.) concept of Arab nationalism is not the total Arab political unity often advocated by the more radical Arab nationalists, but rather a strong cultural, social, economic, and security relationship among the various Arab states and peoples that makes the whole more than the sum of its parts.

ARAB REVOLT. *See* INTRODUCTION: JORDAN'S HISTORY, ABDULLAH IBN HUSSEIN, FAISAL IBN HUSSEIN, GREAT BRITAIN, HASHEMITES, OTTOMAN EMPIRE.

ARAB SUMMITS. From time to time, the heads of Arab states hold summit meetings. Jordan hosted two of these summits in the 1980s. Decisions taken at these meetings have frequently had important consequences for Jordan. The 1964 summit decisions and subsequent actions were contributing causes of the 1967 Arab-Israeli war, during which Jordan lost the West Bank to Israel. In 1974 the Rabat summit declared the Palestinian Liberation Organization (q.v.) to be the sole legitimate representative of the Palestinian people, a declaration that undermined Jordan politically. In 1978 the Baghdad summit voted funds for those Arab States which were in confrontation with Israel, including Jordan. While Jordan has benefited from this largess it has actually collected less than half of the promised funds. In addition, the Jordanian-Palestinian Joint Committee (q.v.) was established to administer funds pledged at the summit for projects in the West Bank and Gaza. *See also* WARS.

ARABIC. Arabic is the official language of Jordan. The written language is virtually the same throughout the Arab world. The spoken language in Jordan falls within the general dialect of eastern Mediterranean Arabic. In Jordan there are slight variations in the spoken language between the rural and urban areas and between the Palestinians and Jordanians. The influence of television, radio, and education has caused many of these differences to moderate or disappear.

ARAFAT, YASSER (1929–   ). Yasser Arafat is chairman of the Palestine Liberation Organization (q.v.). In the mid-1960s, he founded Fatah (q.v.), the strongest guerrilla group in the PLO, and he still leads it. Because Jordan's history is integrally related to that of the Palestinians, Yasser Arafat has necessarily played an important role in that country. He led guerrilla raids from Jordan into Israel in the late 1960s. He was involved in the Jordanian-Palestinian strife in 1970, which culminated in Black September's (q.v.) fighting when the Jordan Arab Army defeated the Palestinian forces in Amman and throughout the country. During the 1980s, the relations between Yasser Arafat and King Hussein have been strained, with occasional periods of political rapprochement. *See also* ARAB-ISRAELI CONFLICT, PALESTINE, PALESTINIANS, WEST BANK.

ARMENIANS. Armenians are a small ethnic Christian minority in Jordan. Most belong to the Armenian Orthodox church, but a few adhere to the Armenian Catholic rite. They often speak their own language among themselves, but they use Arabic in public. *See also* CHRISTIANS.

ASSAD, HAFEZ AL- (1930–). Hafez al-Assad has been president of Syria (q.v.) since 1970. As head of the Syrian air force in September 1970, he did not bring Syrian air power to bear in the Jordanian-Syrian clashes during that month. In the mid-1970s, King Hussein (q.v.) and Jordan enjoyed good political and economic relations with Assad's Syria. However, by the late 1970s, these relations had deteriorated due to ideological and regional rivalry.

ASSEMBLY OF NOTABLES. The Assembly of Notables, a body appointed by Amir Abdullah (q.v.), sat from 1926 to 1928. In its meetings, the members stimulated the writing of Jordan's first constitution—the Organic law—and the first Jordanian electoral law.

ASSYRIANS. The Assyrian Orthodox, or Nestorians, are a small Christian sect in Jordan. Their church services are in Syriac and some members of the group speak the language. *See also* CHRISTIANS.

AWQAF. In Jordan, the Awqaf is the Muslim Religious Foundation. It is administered by the Ministry of Awqaf, Islamic Affairs and Holy Places. In Arabic *awqaf* is plural of *waqf* which means religious "endowment."

AYYUBIDS. The Ayyubid dynasty, started by Saladin in the late twelfth century, ruled Jordan and neighboring areas until it was defeated by the Mamluks in 1260.

AZRAQ. Azraq is an oasis in the northeastern Jordanian desert. Two villages, Azraq al-Druz and Azraq al-Shishani are located there. The economy is based on salt panning, trade with the bedouin (q.v.) and pumping water to Zarqa (q.v.). Historically, Azraq is known for the ruins of an Umayyad castle. This structure served as the headquarters for T. E. Lawrence (q.v.) during the period when he was advising the military leaders of the Arab Revolt during World War I.

B

BAGHDAD PACT. In 1955 Iran, Iraq (q.v.), and Turkey joined with Britain in a mutual defense treaty, popularly known as the Baghdad Pact. Because the United States was courting Egypt and Saudi Arabia at the time, and these two states were strongly opposed to the pact, the United States did not become a full member of the treaty group. However, the United States did support its goals of containing the Soviet Union and communism. In 1955 Jordan was pressed very strongly to become a member of the Baghdad Pact, and young King Hussein (q.v.), it is thought, wanted to join. Inter alia, financial and military assistance was being offered through this mechanism. However, the forces of Arab nationalism (q.v.) defeated it on the streets of Amman and provincial capitals.

BALFOUR DECLARATION. The Balfour Declaration is salient to Jordan because in many ways Jordan's importance in the world is defined by its neighbors to the west: Israel (q.v.) and the Palestinians (q.v.). The issuance of the Balfour Declaration is one of the key events leading to the creation of Israel. During World War I, Great Britain's (q.v.) Foreign Secretary Arthur James Balfour wrote a letter, dated November 1917, to the Zionist leader Lord Lionel Rothschild in which he declared that the British government viewed with favor "the establishment in Palestine of a national home for the Jewish people." In addition, the civil and religious rights of the existing non-Jewish communities (the Palestinians) would not be prejudiced. In the ensuing years, thousands of Jewish immigrants arrived, primarily from Europe. This influx resulted in conflict between the Jews and the local Palestinian Arab population that the British mandatory rulers could barely contain. Amir Abdullah and Jordan, though neighbors, were largely removed from these developments until the creation of Israel in 1948. Subsequent to this date, though, Jordan has been integrally involved in the Arab-Israeli conflict, a linear product of the Balfour Declaration. *See also* ARAB-ISRAELI CONFLICT, PALESTINE.

BA'TH PARTY. The Ba'th is a radical Arab nationalist party, two branches of which currently rule in Syria and Iraq. While not legal in Jordan, it has long had members in that country. In the 1950s and 1960s, it was considerably more active on the streets and in people's minds than it has been during the current decade. *See also* ARAB NATIONALISM.

BEDOUIN. The true bedouin, according to the classic definition, are the nomads who depend mostly upon camels rather than sheep and goats for their livelihood, live in black (goat-hair) tents, and do not settle in permanent houses. As history has evolved, however, in Jordan the bedouin are now largely but not entirely settled and somewhat resemble sedentary villagers (fellahs) (q.v.), while retaining a legacy of bedouin customs and practices. The bedouin sociopolitical groupings are called tribes, *qabila* (pl., *qaba'il*), in Arabic.

Jordan is often described as a bedouin country or, at least, originally a bedouin country. Neither depiction is correct, but the bedouin have enjoyed a strong social, cultural, and political role in the country. In the early years of the amirate, the bedouin were less than 40% of the population. In the early 1990s, they make up less than 5%. The bedouin, though, have contributed considerably to the maintenance of the Hashemite (q.v.) throne. Once the bedouin loyalty to the regime was secured in the early 1930s, they provided strong political and military support in both calm periods and in times of crisis. This support has been expressed primarily through bedouin service in the army (known as the Arab Legion [q.v.] from 1921 to 1956 and the Jordan Arab Army [q.v.] from 1956 on), which has had a significant bedouin contingent since 1930, especially in the more sensitive positions. From a social and cultural perspective, the Jordanians also often idealize bedouin customs, saying that the bedouin are the model from which other Jordanian patterns are derived.

Those who maintain the bedouin style of life live primarily in the eastern two-thirds of Jordan, a desert area called the Badia, a word derived from the Arabic word for bedouin. During the dry months of the year, those bedouin who still retain a nomadic mode of existence move their encampments closer to the more settled highland areas in search of water and pasturage. The most important Jordanian bedouin tribes are the Huwaytat and the Bani Sukhur. Other large bedouin tribes are the Bani Atiya, Sirhan, Bani Khalid, and Rwala. Parts of two Palestinian tribes took refuge in Jordan after 1948: the Azazma and Jaraba. *See also* TRIBES AND KINSHIP.

BLACK SEPTEMBER. During the "Black" September of 1970, Jordanian army troops clashed with Palestinian guerrillas in Amman and throughout Jordan. After severe fighting during which many Palestinians (q.v.) and some Jordanians lost their lives, the Palestinian guerrillas were driven out of Jordan. During the same period, Syrian tanks invaded Jordan across its northern border. They were defeated by the Jordanian army and air force. Subsequently a special Palestinian guerrilla group was named after this period. It is noteworthy, however, that despite the fact that most of the fighting was between the Jordanian military and the Palestinian guerrillas, the large majority of the Palestinians in the Jordan Arab Army remained loyal to the throne. *See also* ARAFAT, FATAH, PALESTINE LIBERATION ORGANIZATION, PALESTINIANS.

BRITAIN. *See* GREAT BRITAIN.

BYZANTINE EMPIRE. In A.D. 330 the Roman Empire shifted its capital to Byzantium (Constantinople) and shortly thereafter converted to Christianity under Emperor Constantine. The evolving empire eventually came to be known as the Byzantine Empire and its rule encompassed, among other areas, the Fertile Crescent (q.v.), including Jordan. Between A.D. 629 and 636, the Arab Muslims invaded the Fertile Crescent, ending Byzantine rule in that area.

C

CABINET (COUNCIL OF MINISTERS). *See* GOVERNMENT.

CAMP DAVID ACCORDS. The Camp David Accords were negotiated by Egypt, Israel, and the United States in 1978. They were to be the framework for the settlement of the Arab-Israeli conflict (q.v.). One part dealt with the Sinai and the establishment of peaceful relations between Egypt and Israel. In 1979 this part of the accords was realized when the peace treaty was signed, and over the following years its terms were fulfilled. The other part consisted of a complex series of steps to be taken with respect to the West Bank (q.v.) and Gaza (q.v.), among which was a period of autonomy and eventual negotiations about the future of the West Bank and Gaza, the results of which were to be approved by all parties to the conflict. Jordan was given a significant role in the second part of the Camp David Accords. However, during the negotiations, Jordan was not consulted. Its opinions and input were not sought. Consequent to this and to the Jordanian consideration that the formulations in the Camp David Accords were not in its best interests, the Jordanian government declined to participate in the Camp David process. *See also* EGYPT, ISRAEL.

CARTER, PRESIDENT JIMMY (1924–   ) . President Carter was a primary architect of the Camp David Accords (q.v.). During his presidency (1977–1981) United States relations with Jordan remained friendly, but were not close.

CHAMBER OF DEPUTIES (PARLIAMENT). *See* GOVERNMENT, PARLIAMENT.

CHRISTIANS. Christianity has a long history in Jordan, dating back almost to the origins of the religion. According to the Bible, Jesus Christ was baptized in the Jordan River (q.v.). In the East Bank of the Jordan, about 125,000 Christians live in and around the provincial towns of Karak, Madaba, and Salt, as well as in the capital of Amman. In the West Bank, significant numbers live in Jerusalem, Bethlehem, and Ramallah. The largest Jordanian Christian group is the Greek Orthodox, about two-thirds of the total. The balance is divided among Greek Catholics, Roman Catholics, Protestants, Armenian Orthodox, Assyrians, and Syrian Orthodox. The latter three groups are not ethnically Arab, but are members of their own ethnic groups.

CHURCHILL, WINSTON (1874–1965). Amir Abdullah (q.v.) met then Colonial Secretary Winston Churchill in Jerusalem on March 27, 1921. At this meeting, Great Britain agreed to accept Abdullah as the leader, or amir, of Jordan. In exchange, Amir Abdullah agreed not to pursue his Greater Syria (q.v.) ambitions. In addition, Jordan was removed from the Palestine mandate and given separate terms with its own mandate, later recorded at the San Remo Conference, which regularized and recognized the various mandates. *See also* INTRODUCTION: JORDAN'S HISTORY, GREAT BRITAIN.

CIRCASSIANS. The Circassians are a small ethnic Muslim minority that came to the Jordanian region from Caucasia in the 1880s. They number about 25,000 and are concentrated in Amman and Sweilih. Although they are not a politically assertive group, due to their loyalty to the Hashemites they enjoy a disproportionately high number of positions in government, military, and security forces.

CIVIL WAR. *See* INTRODUCTION: JORDAN'S HISTORY, BLACK SEPTEMBER, PALESTINIANS.

COMMUNIST PARTY. Like many Middle East countries, Jordan has a small Communist party. It, like all other political parties in Jordan with the exception of the Muslim Brotherhood, is illegal. The government, though, pays special attention to its members. Many have served long jail terms, and they are frequently arrested during periods of crackdown.

COOPERATIVES. The cooperatives, both rural and urban, are one of the most important sets of organizations in the country. Through these organizations, people join together to solve common economic problems. The cooperative movement was started in 1952, and with occasional external assistance, has grown significantly since that time.

For example, agricultural cooperative members alone numbered 12,000 in 1980. In a country without active political organizations, the cooperatives take on added meaning and at times are the nexus for grass-roots leadership. *See also* JORDAN COOPERATIVE ORGANIZATION.

COUNCIL OF MINISTERS (CABINET). *See* GOVERNMENT.

COUNCIL OF NOTABLES. *See* GOVERNMENT, SENATE.

CRUSADERS. In the late eleventh century, parts of Jordan, Palestine, and Lebanon fell to the Christian Crusaders from Europe. Historically and religiously, the region was central to both Christianity and Islam. For the former, Christ lived and taught around Jerusalem. For Islam, Jerusalem is one of its three holy cities, the site of the Prophet Muhammad's ascension to heaven on his faithful steed Buraq. In Jordan, the Crusader Renard de Châtillon ruled from Karak in ancient Moab, where he built a magnificent fortress that still stands. In 1099 the Crusaders conquered Jerusalem, but in 1187 they were defeated by the Muslim leader Saladin (Salah al-Din) (q.v.). One consequence of the Crusader era was that many local Arab Christians converted to Islam. Also, in some localities, blond hair and blue eyes are not uncommon because of intermarriage and the taking of many European slaves. *See also* CHRISTIANS, ISLAM.

D

DEAD SEA. One of the most striking features of Jordan is the Dead Sea, which at 1,296 feet (395 meters) below sea level, is the lowest point on earth. Israel and the West Bank also border the Dead Sea. Aside from its topographical uniqueness, the Dead Sea is an economic asset. It is a tourist attraction, and potash (q.v.) is extracted from its very briny waters.

DEVELOPMENT. Development, both social and economic, has been a central concern in Jordan since the country gained its independence after World War II. The process was directed by the National Planning Council (q.v.) until this was replaced by the Ministry of Planning in the 1980s. King Hussein (q.v.) and his brother, Crown Prince Hassan (q.v.), have taken considerable interest in the development process. The king's efforts at acquiring resources from outside Jordan have been crucial for its success. And Prince Hassan is integrally involved in planning, promotion, and publicity for the process. The Jordanian people, too, are involved. Development is often a subject of conversation as well as action. It is frequently featured on television and in the newspapers.

The results of this decades-long development process are manifest. Literacy, especially among the younger generations, is widespread. Universities and polytechnic institutions have been built and staffed. Health standards have been raised: for example the number of hospital beds per thousand people is similar to that in the United States. Looking at development from another perspective, twenty years ago there was a stark contrast between urban and rural standards, the former enjoying many more basic amenities (such as running water, electricity, and government services). Today those differences have largely, but not entirely, disappeared. In towns 99% of the homes have electricity; in the villages the figure is 81%. The data for running water are 92% and 78% respectively. With the introduction of a large-scale irrigation system in the Jordan Valley (q.v.), agricultural production has soared. With respect to industry, even though some large facilities relating to phosphates, potash, cement, and petroleum refining have been constructed, industrial labor constitutes only a small proportion of the work force.

Reflecting the general economic downturn in the Middle East from the mid-1980s, Jordan's economy has declined in recent years. While many of the gains noted above have not been lost, employment opportunities have suffered and the Jordan dinar was devalued. *See also* ECONOMY.

E

EAST BANK. The East Bank is that land of Jordan which lies to the east of the Jordan River and the Wadi al-Araba. Since June 1967, it is the only territory that the government in Amman controls. Historically, the East Bank was called Transjordan, or Trans-Jordan. In 1950 the East Bank and the West Bank (q.v.) joined together as the Hashemite Kingdom of Jordan. In this dictionary, when the word *Jordan* is used, the East Bank is being referred to in the pre-1950 period and the period after 1967. During the 1950–1967 period, *Jordan* refers to both the East and West Banks. Many texts on Jordan refer to the East Bank as East Jordan.

EAST GHOR CANAL. The East Ghor Canal runs virtually the entire length of the Jordan Valley and is the primary water carrier for the valley's comprehensive irrigation scheme. (*Al-ghor* is the Arabic word for the Jordan Valley.) The canal's waters come from the Yarmuk River, the Zarqa River, and small tributaries. The primary canal was completed in 1964. It was damaged by shelling from Israel (aimed at Palestinian guerrillas) in the 1967–1970 period and repaired in the early 1970s. When (and if) the Maqarin Dam on the Yarmuk River is finished, the canal's water flow will be increased substantially. *See also* AGRICUL-

TURE, JORDAN VALLEY, JORDAN VALLEY AUTHORITY, MAQARIN DAM.

EAST JORDAN. East Jordan is the East Bank (q.v.).

ECONOMY. From the late 1940s, development (q.v.) has been the watchword of Jordan's economy. Starting from a very modest base, it grew by 11% per year from 1954 to 1967. After a period of contraction due to wars, civil strife, and international and regional pressures, it resumed healthy growth in 1974, but by the mid-1980s, along with the Middle East economy generally, it slowed to the point of stagnation. Jordan's developing economy is marked by its dependence on the larger economy of the Middle East and on bilateral and multilateral economic assistance from outside the country.

In terms of both the labor force and share of gross national product (GNP), Jordan's economy is dominated by the service sector, followed by mining and manufacturing, agriculture, and construction. The economy is highly skewed in the direction of the service sector because of Jordan's artificially high population due to the presence of Palestinian (q.v.) refugees, the very high birthrate, the elevated number of government employees in both the civilian and military sectors, and the government's successful efforts at extending essential services throughout the country. The figures on labor force and GNP distribution are found in Table 1. In addition 277,000 Jordanians work in oil-rich Middle Eastern countries.

Jordan's economy may be characterized as a free enterprise system. The government, through its access to financial resources, does play a considerable role through investment as well as through the regulation of some prices, the provision of subsidies for staples, and restrictions on imports. In 1988 the Jordan dinar, considered to be overvalued by the international community, was devalued by

Table 1. Jordan's Labor Force and Gross National Product [1]

Sector	Labor Force	%	Gross National Product	%
Agriculture	37,736	7.4	127.2	8.3
Mining & Manufacture	62,092	12.2	297.9	19.5
Construction	53,360	10.5	101.3	6.6
Services	356,156	69.9	1,000.6	65.6
TOTAL	509,344		1,527.0	

[1] By sector in terms of workers and Jordanian dinars, respectively (1987).

40%. This action helped stimulate the export of agricultural and manufactured products, but made imports more expensive for the people, resulting in an economic crisis in 1988 and 1989. The Persian Gulf Crisis and War (q.v.) of 1990–91 severely exacerbated the downturn.

The only extractive industries of any consequence are phosphate (q.v.) and potash (q.v.), both of which are used in fertilizers. Phosphate mining was developed in the 1960s and significantly expanded in the late 1970s. Potash is extracted from the mineral-rich waters of the Dead Sea (q.v.). An expensive and sophisticated technology, it was not introduced in Jordan until the 1980s. Heavy industry is limited to fertilizer and cement plants and a petroleum refinery. Smaller industries produce pharmaceutical products, ceramics, textiles, cigarettes, shoes, detergents, batteries, and foodstuffs.

Jordan's landmass is dominated by desert; only 3% of its surface is cultivated. The main products of the irrigated Jordan Valley are vegetables and citrus, part of which is exported. In the highlands, fruit trees and grains are cultivated, but Jordan is only 50% self-sufficient in wheat production. In the marginal areas next to the desert, the bedouin and peasants practice animal husbandry. Chicken factories and sheep feedlots were introduced in the 1970s. Land is broadly distributed among the farming population, most farms being of small or medium size: 75% of holdings—almost 75% of the land—is farmed by owners. Cultivation practices are increasingly modern, especially in the highly developed Jordan Valley. This modernization has contributed to the decline—50% in the last 15 years—in farm labor as a proportion of the total labor force.

Service industries dominate the Jordanian economy. Education, military, health, transportation, trade, and government are the main constituents of this sector. In the last two decades, more than a quarter of a million Jordanians from this sector have traveled to Kuwait, Saudi Arabia, and the United Arab Emirates to find work. They contribute to the Jordanian economy by sending remittances to their families in Jordan. During the Persian Gulf Crisis many returned to the country.

Jordan is almost entirely dependent on importation for its energy resources. One dam produces some electricity; otherwise oil is used to generate power for Jordan's national grid, which now covers most of the country. In some more traditional villages charcoal, wood, and animal dung are still used as fuel.

Jordan's primary exports are phosphates, potash, vegetables, fruit, and some light manufactured products. Less conventionally, Jordan also exports educated, trained people. The markets are primarily in the Middle East and other Third World countries. Jordan's imports—petroleum, grain, meat, and manufactured consumer items—come from Saudi Arabia, the United States, Europe, and Japan.

Jordan has a well-developed transportation system. Its paved highways link it with all its neighbors. A railroad runs from Syria through Jordan to Saudi Arabia, with a major spur to Jordan's only port at Aqaba on the Red Sea with access to the Indian Ocean. International carriers and

Jordan's own airline serve the modern airport outside Amman. *See also* DEVELOPMENT.

EDUCATION.   Education is popular throughout Jordan among most socioeconomic sectors of the society. Schooling is compulsory through the ninth grade, and the law is largely followed. Seventy percent of the pupils are in government schools, 22% in those run by the United Nations Relief and Works Agency for Palestine Refugees, the U.N. agency that serves Palestinian (q.v.) refugees, and the balance are in private schools. At successful graduation from twelfth grade (which involves passing a national exam), a student earns the *tawjihi*, a highly valued degree that helps open up many employment opportunities. Community colleges, vocational schools, and polytechnic institutions have increased greatly in the last two decades. They now have 46,000 students. Jordan also has four universities with 28,500 students—in Amman (the oldest), Irbid (two), and Karak. A larger number attend university in other Arab countries, Europe, and the United States. Until the early 1980s, all graduates easily found employment, but this has become more difficult in recent years with the increasing number of graduates and the economic downturn in the Middle East. Looking at education from a more basic level, 75% of the population are literate (illiteracy is primarily among the elderly and women) and 52% have at least a primary school certificate.

EGYPT. Egypt, an Arab country located to the southwest of Jordan in North Africa, has been both a friend and nemesis of Jordan. In 1948 the Egyptian government, then under King Farouk, strongly objected to Amir Abdullah's acquiring the West Bank. During the 1950s and 1960s, one of the most difficult challenges faced by young King Hussein and Jordan was radical Arab nationalism (q.v.), charismatically led by Egypt's President, Gamel Abdel Nasser (q.v.), and occasional attempts at direct Egyptian subversion in Jordan. Jordan has enjoyed much closer relations with Egypt during the presidencies of Anwar Sadat and Hosni Mubarak. Although Jordan joined most other Arab countries in severing diplomatic relations with Egypt following the signing of the Egyptian-Israeli peace treaty, Jordan was the first Arab country to reestablish these ties. In 1988 Jordan joined with Egypt, Iraq, and North Yemen to form the Arab Cooperation Council. Through this council, the countries are to cooperate politically and economically for their mutual benefit. The Persian Gulf Crisis and War (q.v.), though, rendered the council moribund.

EISENHOWER DOCTRINE. On January 5, 1957, President Eisenhower issued the Eisenhower Doctrine. In this doctrine, the United States pledged to aid Middle Eastern countries against Soviet aggression and subversion. Jordan did not formally approve this doctrine; however under its general umbrella, King Hussein (q.v.) developed close relations with the United States (q.v.). In some ways, these ties replaced those with Jordan's former mandatory power, Great Britain (q.v.).

F

FAISAL IBN HUSSEIN, KING. King Faisal, son of Sharif Hussein ibn Ali (q.v.) of Mecca, was born in that city in 1885. He was the military leader of the great Arab Revolt against the Ottoman Empire during World War I. Many of the battles were fought in what is now Jordan. At the end of World War I, he established an Arab government in Damascus and was crowned king of what was officially called the United Syrian Kingdom in 1920. Jordan fell under the rule of this government and sent delegates to the General Syrian Congress, an Arab parliament, in Damascus. In July 1920, France militarily drove him out of Damascus, ending the United Syrian Kingdom (q.v.), and established its own mandate in Syria. The British in 1921 made Faisal king of one of their other Arab mandates, Iraq. Also in that year, his brother, Abdullah (q.v.), became amir of the new British mandate of Jordan (Transjordan). King Faisal died in 1933. *See also* HASHEMITES.

FATAH. Fatah is the largest Palestinian guerrilla group. It was founded by Yasser Arafat (q.v.) in the 1960s. Since about 1970, it has been the strongest group within the Palestine Liberation Organization (q.v.). It was involved in the Palestinian-Jordanian fighting in 1970 and retains a small representational presence in Jordan to this day.

FELLAH. *Fellah* means "peasant" or "tiller of the soil" in Arabic. In Jordan, virtually all sedentary villagers call themselves fellahs. It is a term of identification, as distinct from bedouin or city dweller. *See also* BEDOUIN, TRIBES AND KINSHIP.

FERTILE CRESCENT. The Fertile Crescent refers to the geographical arc starting from southern Jordan and Palestine, stretching through Lebanon and western and northern Syria, and continuing through the Tigris and Euphrates valleys of Iraq. This is the arable land of the Middle East. The land partially encircled by the arc and Arabia to its south—the Great Syrian Desert and the Arabian Desert respectively—are not hospitable to agriculture.

FLAG. The Jordanian flag has three horizontal bands of black, white and green joined at the staff by a red triangle with a white star in the middle. The flag of the Arab Revolt against the Ottoman Empire led by the Hashemites was identical, but without the star.

G

GAZA. Gaza, often referred to as the Gaza Strip, is a small segment of Palestine (q.v.). Its borders to the north and east are with Israel, to the south with Egypt, and to the west with the Mediterranean Sea. In 1948 the Gaza Strip was occupied and then administered by Egypt. Since 1967 Gaza has been militarily occupied by Israel. In 1986 it was included in the Jordan Development Program for the Palestinians in the Israeli-occupied territories. The program was canceled in 1988. *See also* ARAB-ISRAELI CONFLICT.

GHASSANIDS. The Ghassanid Arab tribe established its presence and gained control over Jordan and neighboring regions in ca. A.D. 200. Operating under the suzerainty of the Roman Empire, the tribe converted to Christianity in ca. A.D. 330 during the reign of Emperor Constantine. The Ghassanids continued to hold sway in Jordan during the Byzantine period until the region was conquered by the Arab Muslims in A.D. 629–636.

GHOR. *See* JORDAN VALLEY.

GLUBB, JOHN BAGOT (1897–1983). Major John Glubb, a British officer, came to Jordan in 1930 to establish a special bedouin unit within the Arab Legion (q.v.); in 1939 he was appointed commander of the entire force. Glubb, who soon became a general, was instrumental in developing the Arab Legion, which was to play a crucial role in the affairs of the state. Under his command, it helped Jordan acquire the West Bank in 1948. It also provided crucial internal security during volatile periods in the kingdom. In 1956 King Hussein dismissed General Glubb as Jordan sought to Arabize the army's officer corps. At that time, the Arab Legion became the Jordan Arab Army. Glubb authored many books on Jordan and the Arab Legion.

GOVERNMENT. Jordan is a constitutional monarchy. The head of state is the king, currently Hussein ibn Talal (q.v.), in whom the executive powers of the kingdom are vested. He signs and executes all laws, and appoints and dismisses the Council of Ministers (cabinet) and all judges. The prime minister (q.v.)—the leader of the cabinet—is the head of government. The cabinet is responsible to an elected parliament. With a two-thirds vote, that body may dismiss the cabinet.

Legislative power is in the bicameral National Assembly composed of the Chamber of Deputies (parliament) (q.v.), which is elected by universal suffrage for a four-year term, and a Senate, or Council of Notables, appointed by the king. Due to the loss of the West Bank in 1967 (where half of the parliament's members were to be elected), nationwide elections were not held until 1989. In the interim, the parliament was dissolved in 1974, recalled in 1984, but dismissed again in 1988. The current parliament, elected in November 1989, continues to hold periodic sessions.

The country is divided into eight governorates. Governors are appointed by the crown; they in turn are the authority for the various government departments in their jurisdictions. They are responsible for developmental projects, but the Ministry of Planning also plays a crucial role. With respect to the judiciary, there are three kinds of courts: civil, religious, and special. The first deals with commercial and criminal law; religious courts regulate personal status (such as marriage, inheritance, and orphans); and special courts deal with such areas as customs or tribal affairs.

GREAT BRITAIN. Britain has had a close relationship with Jordan throughout the latter's history as a distinct geographical and political entity. During World War I, Britain assisted the great Arab Revolt against the Ottoman Empire which, inter alia, led to the establishment of the Amirate of Transjordan (Jordan). Upon its establishment, Jordan became a British mandate under the League of Nations. In the 1946–1948 period, Jordan gained a significant degree of independence from Britain and, as Britain withdrew from its Palestine mandate, Jordan acquired the West Bank, that part of Palestine west of the Jordan River. The Arab Legion (q.v.) was founded with the help of the British in the early 1920s. Its senior officers came from Britain from its founding until 1956, when it was renamed the Jordan Arab Army and its officer corps was Arabized. By the late 1950s, Jordan had severed the bulk of its preindependence, or mandatory, ties with Britain. Nevertheless, Jordan has maintained close relations with Britain due to this colonial legacy as well as the moderate, relatively pro-Western outlook of Jordan and its leadership. *See also* INTRODUCTION: JORDAN'S HISTORY.

GREATER SYRIA. Greater Syria is one of the Arab nationalist concepts, which advocates that the lands of Syria, Lebanon, Palestine, and Jordan (and some include Iraq) should all be united in one political unit. The short-lived United Syrian Kingdom (q.v.), which included Jordan and which was based in Damascus during the year of 1920, was an early embodiment of the concept. Amir Abdullah (q.v.), when he traveled to Jordan in late 1920 was again trying to realize this concept. Throughout his reign in Jordan, Amir (later King) Abdullah spoke about Greater Syria and Arab nationalism in one form or another. When Jordan acquired the West Bank (q.v.), the concept was again partially realized.

GREEK CATHOLIC. The Greek Catholics are a small Christian sect in Jordan. *See also* CHRISTIANS.

GREEK ORTHODOX. The Greek Orthodox are the largest Christian sect in Jordan. *See also* CHRISTIANS.

GROSS NATIONAL PRODUCT (GNP). *See* ECONOMY.

GUERRILLAS. *See* FATAH, PALESTINE LIBERATION ORGANIZATION, POPULAR FRONT FOR THE LIBERATION OF PALESTINE.

H

HASHEMITE KINGDOM OF JORDAN. The Hashemite Kingdom of Jordan is the official name of the country of Jordan.

HASHEMITES. The Hashemites are a notable family of Arabia with origins in Mecca that can be traced back to the time of the Prophet Muhammad. Hashem, a scion of the distinguished Quraish clan of Mecca and the founder of the Hashemite family, was the Prophet Muhammad's great-grandfather and by tradition then Amir, later King, Abdullah (q.v.) and King Hussein (q.v.) are direct descendants of the Prophet through his daughter, Fatima. In recent times, the Hashemites have again played a historic role in the Middle East. By the mid-nineteenth century they were considered to be the most prominent religious and political family in Mecca, the capital of the Hejaz and center of Muslim pilgrimage. In 1908 Sultan Abdul Hamid II appointed the Hashemite leader Sharif (q.v.) Hussein ibn Ali (q.v.) Amir (q.v.) of Mecca. From this base, Sharif Hussein and his very able sons, in league with the British but in the name of Arab nationalism, led the great Arab Revolt against the Ottoman Empire during World War I.

At the resolution of this conflict, Ali, the grand sharif's eldest son and heir apparent, remained in Mecca. In Damascus, his second son, Faisal (q.v.), was originally made viceroy with responsibility for Syria and Jordan. And in 1920 the General Syrian Congress declared him king of the United Kingdom of Syria. However, basing its action on the secret wartime Franco-British Sykes-Picot Agreement, the French army soon removed him. The British then installed him as king of Iraq. Following these events, Abdullah, Sharif Hussein's third son and grandfather of King Hussein, entered Jordan with the intent of marching to Damascus to reclaim the throne for the Hashemites. Thwarted in this aim, in 1921 he became Amir of Jordan with the acquiescence of the British.

Thus for a brief period, Hashemites ruled the Hejaz, Iraq, and Jordan. In 1925 Amir Ali who had replaced his father in Mecca, lost the throne to the forces of the House of Saud as the Kingdom of Saudi Arabia (q.v.) was being pieced together in the Arabian Peninsula. The young King Faisal II, grandson of Faisal I, was killed in 1958 as the Hashemite rule in Iraq was terminated. Consequently, by mid-1958, King Hussein was the only remaining Hashemite monarch. *See also* HUSSEIN IBN TALAL.

HASSAN IBN TALAL, H.R.H. CROWN PRINCE. C r o w n Prince Hassan, born in 1948, is the youngest brother of King Hussein (q.v.) and son of King Talal (q.v.). Educated at Oxford University in Britain, he is known as the more intellectual of Talal's sons. He has written a number of books on Arab and Jordanian subjects. In 1965 he was named crown prince. His older brother, Muhammad, was passed over because he suffers from schizophrenia as did his father, Talal. Aside from serving as regent in the absence of his brother, the king, Crown Prince Hassan has taken a strong lead in the social and economic development process. He frequently holds meetings that address development issues.

HEJAZ RAILROAD. From 1900 through 1908 the Hejaz Railroad was built from what is now Turkey through Jordan to the area surrounding Mecca. While it made Jordan only marginally more important, economically it was very important for the region. During the Arab Revolt against the Ottoman Empire (q.v.) during World War I, the Arab forces assisted by the British officer T. E. Lawrence (q.v.)

spent considerable effort to disrupt the railroad and impede the Ottoman's military use of it.

HUSSEIN, SADDAM (1937–   ). Saddam Hussein has been president of Iraq (q.v.) from the 1970s until the time of this writing, 1991. Even though Saddam Hussein is a product of the radical Arab nationalist Ba'th Party (q.v.), he and King Hussein (q.v.) have generally enjoyed positive relations. King Hussein strongly supported Iraq in its war with Iran throughout the 1980s. In August 1990, Saddam Hussein's Iraq invaded and occupied Kuwait, precipitating the Persian Gulf Crisis and War (q.v.) of 1990–91.

HUSSEIN IBN ALI, SHARIF. Sharif Hussein, scion of the notable Hashemite family, was born in Mecca in 1852. He spent many of his formative years in Istanbul, the capital of the Ottoman Empire (q.v.). In 1908 Sultan Abdul Hamid II appointed Sharif Hussein, whom he thought to be loyal to the Ottoman Empire, Amir of Mecca. From this base, Sharif Hussein and his very able sons (Ali, Faisal [q.v.], and Abdullah [q.v.]), in league with the British, but in the name of Arab nationalism (q.v.), led the great Arab Revolt against the Ottoman Empire during World War I. His son Abdullah became Amir of Jordan and his son Faisal became King of Iraq, both in 1921. Ali replaced his father as the grand sharif of Mecca in 1924, but lost the city and the Hejaz to the Saud family as it was piecing together the Kingdom of Saudi Arabia (q.v.). Sharif Hussein died in 1931. *See also* HASHEMITES, SHARIF.

HUSSEIN IBN TALAL, H.R.M. KING. As a member of the notable Hashemite (q.v.) family, H.R.M. King Hussein ibn Talal enjoys a rich, noble heritage. In 1991, at the time of this writing, he enjoys the record of being the longest-ruling head of state in the world. Many had predicted that his rule would not last, that the very country of Jordan would not last. However, he, his grandfather King Abdullah (q.v.), and the Jordanian people have proved the prediction wrong. But the path to national and regime longevity has not always been easy.

When King Hussein was born in 1935, the Amirate of Jordan had existed for only fourteen years. At the time, Talal ibn Abdullah (q.v.), King Hussein's father, was crown prince. His mother, Zein, was from a collateral branch of the Hashemite family. Due to Talal's ill health—he was schizophrenic—the Jordanian leadership realized that Prince Hussein would be the next actual inheritor of the throne. Consequently, his grandfather, then Amir Abdullah, personally tutored him in statecraft.

Despite his immediate family's meager means, he was provided a broad education at appropriate schools. In Amman his classes at an Islamic school and the Bishop's School were augmented by special tutorials in Arabic and religion. Later, he attended the prestigious Victoria College in Alexandria where he expanded his world view. Following his grandfather's assassination in 1951, Prince Hussein's education was shifted to England where he joined his cousin, Crown Prince Faisal of Iraq, at Harrow, an elite school for future leaders of Britain and the British Empire.

King Hussein's life again changed on August 11, 1952, when due to illness, the Jordanian Parliament relieved King Talal of his duties and passed the crown to Prince Hussein. Not having reached his majority, a regency council ruled Jordan for a year as the new monarch completed his formal education. He spent his last year of formal instruction at Sandhurst, the British military academy, equivalent to America's West Point. At the end of the year, Prince Hussein returned to Amman where he assumed the throne in May 1953.

King Hussein has had four wives. In 1954 he married Sharifa Dina, a distant and older cousin from Cairo. They proved to be incompatible and divorced after only eighteen months of marriage. In 1961 the king married again, this time to the daughter of a British military attaché, Princess Muna. This marriage ended in divorce in 1972. In 1973 the king married a third time, to Alia Tuqan, the daughter of a prominent Nablus, West Bank, family. This marriage ended tragically in 1977 when Queen Alia died in a helicopter crash. In 1978 King Hussein married a fourth time, to Lisa Halaby, the daughter of Najeeb Halaby, an Arab-American and former chairman of Pan American Airways. By his various marriages, King Hussein has seven daughters and five sons.

Crucial to King Hussein's reign are the qualities that give him legitimacy in the minds of the Jordanians. The weight of these factors varies to some degree among the Jordanian socioeconomic groups. First, having led the Arab Revolt against the Ottoman Empire, the Hashemites have a special claim on the origins of Arab nationalism. King Hussein has clearly inherited this strong feeling for and sense of duty toward the larger Arab nation, which he frequently invokes in his public speeches. His view of Arab nationalism (q.v.), however, is not focused on the search for political unity often called for by other Arab leaders—especially in the 1950s and 1960s—but rather a desire for strong cultural, social, economic, and security relations among the Arab states and peoples that make the whole more than the sum of its parts.

Second, King Hussein also claims legitimacy on the basis of his special relationship to Islam (q.v.), that is, his being a direct descendant of the Prophet Muhammad. This religious relationship and the king's public attentiveness to religious issues and leaders are especially meaningful to the more traditional and religious Jordanians.

A third factor that buttresses the king's legitimacy is the perception that he is honestly interested in and, importantly, capable of delivering on, socioeconomic development (q.v.). Most admit that King Hussein and his brother, Prince Hassan (q.v.), have played crucial roles in creating a favorable climate for development efforts and have been able to secure considerable financial resources to sustain them. From the mid-1970s, Jordanians have increasingly enjoyed the benefits of this development. At the minimum it has helped co-opt many people to the regime, some of whom otherwise might not have been so disposed. For many it has simply increased their loyalty.

The fourth characteristic that reflects on King Hussein's rule is the high degree of personal freedom and security enjoyed by his citizens. When Jordanians compare their lot to that of those in neighboring countries, their situation is viewed quite positively. Basically, as long as a citizen, whether of East Jordanian (q.v.) origin or Palestinian (q.v.), is not threatening the state or causing disorder, he can go about his business without undue interference. There are limitations, though. King Hussein (and Amir Abdullah before him) has not allowed great degrees of political freedom or participation, and the security forces have been known to be very strict. Following the 1989 riots in provincial towns, the regime responded positively to the demands for parliamentary elections and a more open political process.

Fifth, King Hussein's very longevity in the face of adversity and regime challenges helps to create respect. Remarkably, by 1991 his 38 years on the throne make him, as noted above, one of the longest-ruling monarchs and heads of state in the world (Queen Elizabeth of the U.K. surpasses him by six months.). In a sense this durability and success breeds success. A final set of characteristics is that the king is personally attractive, speaks excellent Arabic, enjoys an image of strength of character and physical courage, and has an attractive family with many children. In addition, Jordanians like seeing the leader of their small state dealing on their behalf as an equal with the leaders of the Middle East and the world.

King Hussein's rule is marked by two major historical phases. The first two decades were dominated by crises and threats to the throne stemming from inside and outside the country. Radical Arab nationalism brought riots to the streets, challenges from his own prime minister in 1956 and 1957, destabilization by larger and stronger Arab states, and the devastating loss of the West Bank to Israel in the June 1967 war. While surviving, often relying on the loyal military, King Hussein helped put in place the bases for development. Some of the essential infrastructure was constructed and, most importantly, the school system was built so that the vast majority of the population could attain education (q.v.).

The second phase, starting about 1974, is distinguished by a calmer political situation internal to Jordan, much more rapid development fueled by funds derived from the oil boom in neighboring states, and improved relations with most of Jordan's Arab neighbors in a relatively less radical regional atmosphere. By the beginning of this period, the king and his regime had consolidated and institutionalized their internal control via the security and military forces and had put behind them the tumult caused by the Palestinian guerrilla presence that had dominated the 1968–1971 period. King Hussein's heavy investment in education paid off handsomely as the country was able to provide skilled and educated Arab labor to its rich oil-producing neighbors as well as attract funds for its own development process. Despite his problems with the Palestinians, King Hussein has come to be a respected leader in most Arab capitals. Indeed, he has hosted two Arab summits—1980 and 1987—in Jordan. Even though only in his fifties, King Hussein is seen as an elder statesman of the region.

Another long-term trend in the king's rule is his attempt to be moderate and centrist. As a corollary, he does not seek out enemies, he does not try to make enemies or hold grudges against people. Thus, after times of internal challenge to the throne, his regime has not executed the challengers. Some challengers have been sent to prison or exiled, but many were brought back and given positions of some trust. Nor has the king followed radical or overly conservative social, economic, or cultural policies.

The king's relations with the Arab world follow a similar pattern. As leader of a small country and in accordance with his perception of Arab nationalism, he attempts to maintain positive relations with the other Arab states. Looking at this subject from another viewpoint, the king is following a strategic policy for the survival of his country as he consistently attempts to maintain acceptable ties with a majority of the strong Arab states. Finally, he seeks positive relations with the West, with both the United States and European nations.

I

IBRAHIM PASHA (?–1848). Ibrahim Pasha, son of the Egyptian Khedive Muhammad Ali, was commander of the Egyptian army that conquered and controlled the Levant (q.v.), including Jordan, from 1831 to 1841.

INDUSTRY. *See* ECONOMY.

INTERNATIONAL ORGANIZATIONS. Jordan is a member of several international organizations: the United Nations and several of its specialized and related agencies, including the Food and Agricultural Organization, International Atomic Energy Agency, World Health Organization, World Bank, and the International Monetary Fund; the Organization of the Islamic Conference; INTELSAT; Nonaligned Movement; and the League of Arab States (q.v.).

INTIFADA. The *intifada* is the Palestinian (q.v.) uprising against Israeli military occupation and rule in the West Bank and the Gaza Strip that commenced in December 1987 and continues to the time of this writing. *See also* WEST BANK.

IRAQ. Jordan shares its northeastern border with Iraq. Jordan's relations with this neighbor have been both very close and exceptionally strained. Until 1958 a Hashemite (q.v.) sat on the Iraqi throne. During this period, Jordan and Iraq maintained similar views about the Arab world and their relations with it. As conservative monarchies, they were mutually protecting, especially during the 1950s when radical Arab nationalism (q.v.) was in its ascendancy. After the Iraqi coup of 1958 and the overthrow of the Hashemites in Iraq, relations were marked by strain and enmity. However, by the late 1970s, under Iraqi President Saddam Hussein (q.v.), mutual relations improved. Specifically, King Hussein has strongly supported Iraq in its war with Iran during the 1980s, including the provision of volunteer troops. In 1988 Jordan joined Iraq, Egypt, and North Yemen in the Arab Cooperation Council through which the members are to cooperate politically and economically for their mutual benefit. In August 1990 Iraq precipitated the Persian Gulf Crisis and War (q.v.) when it invaded Kuwait. Jordan did not join the U.S.-led coalition, which expelled Iraq from Kuwait in 1991.

IRBID. Irbid is a provincial capital in the north of Jordan. Two universities were built in the Irbid region during the 1970s and 1980s. Irbid was known in the early days of the Jordanian state to be sympathetic to Syria. This separatist tendency has dissipated over the years.

ISLAM. Jordan is officially a Muslim, or Islamic, country. Ninety-five percent of the people adhere to that faith, and almost all are Sunni, or orthodox, Muslims as opposed to those Muslims who follow Shia Islam. The government supports the established religion through its Ministry of Awqaf (q.v.), Islamic Affairs, and Holy Places. Islam deeply affects the lives of many Jordanians. The five pillars of Islam are important to them. Thus, praying five times a day, attendance at mosque for Friday prayers, fasting during the month of Ramadan, tithing, and the pilgrimage to Mecca are aspired to and practiced by many. In addition, the wave of Islamic fervor that has affected the Middle East for the last two decades has not bypassed Jordan. Some Muslims practice their religion more assiduously and publicly. Religious classes and discussions at mosques are more in demand, and some women dress in modern but modest long coats and head scarves. In the 19889 parliamentary elections, candidates following the Islamic tendency won about 40% of the seats.

ISLAMIC PARTY OF LIBERATION. The Islamic Party of Liberation was active in the Middle East throughout the 1950s and 1960s. It sought to liberate people through the Muslim religion and Arab nationalism. It was active in Jordan, especially in the 1950s, and gained a seat in the chamber of deputies (parliament).

ISRAEL. Jordan shares its western border with Israel. Jordan's relations with Israel may be characterized as highly conflictual, but occasionally cooperative. The uneasy relations arise out of the general Arab-Israeli conflict (q.v.): the conflict of two peoples, the Jews and the Arab Palestinians (q.v.), over one land, the land of Palestine. Jordan is involved as a member of the Arab nation, as a neighbor of Israel, as a claimant to sovereignty over part of the land of Palestine (West Bank) (q.v.), and because a little less than half (45%) of its citizens are of Palestinian origin. Consequently, relations along the borders of Jordan and Israel have often been marked by violence: Israeli military strikes into Jordan, Palestinian guerrilla raids from Jordan into Israel, and war in 1948–1949, 1967, and 1973. In 1967 Jordan lost the West Bank to Israeli military occupation. On the more cooperative side, King Abdullah (q.v.) conducted secret negotiations with Israel with the aim of improving, if not regularizing, relations. It is reported that King Hussein (q.v.) on a number of occasions has also held secret meetings with Israeli leaders. With the exception of the brief 1967–1970 period, Jordan has sought to impede all guerrilla raids from its territory into Israel. Subsequent to 1970, it has largely been successful. After the Israeli military occupation of the West Bank, Jordan allowed the Jordan River (q.v.) bridges to remain open so that Palestinians could come to Jordan for social, economic, governmental, and educational purposes.

Israel's presence makes Jordan more important than it would be if Israel were not situated on its western border. From the Arab perspective, it is convenient that Jordan has to deal directly with that problem, that Jordan is essentially a buffer between them and Israel. From the world perspective, regardless of how a country or group thinks the Arab-Israeli conflict should be resolved, Jordan is in the middle of the picture because of its geographical position. For this reason and by dint of its moderate policies, many funders in the world have given a disproportionate (when the modest size of Jordan's population is taken into consideration) share of economic assistance to Jordan. In addition, Jordan is frequently at the center (or shares the center) in the various proposals for solving the Arab-Israeli conflict.

In 1988 King Hussein took a major decision with respect to Jordan's relationship to the Arab-Israeli conflict. On July 31, he dissolved parliament (q.v.), which had been elected from the West and East Banks in 1967, and officially declared Jordan's political and administrative disengagement from the West Bank. This decision followed a major break with the Palestine Liberation Organization (q.v.) in 1986 and the onset in 1987 of the sustained Palestinian uprising (*intifada*) (q.v.) against the Israeli military occupation in the West Bank and Gaza Strip whereby the local Palestinian population clearly demonstrated its loyalty to the PLO. Aside from recognizing a political reality, the king's actions focused the world's attention on the necessity of solving the Israeli-Palestinian problem between the two parties themselves, not just as a minor part of the Arab-Israeli problem. Thus while Jordan is certainly still a major player in the ongoing conflict, it has removed itself from the central position once ascribed to it.

ISRAELITES. The Israelite Jews ruled part of Palestine (q.v.) for a couple of centuries during biblical times. During 950–850 B.C., they controlled Moab (q.v.) in Jordan, but were driven out by Moabite King Mesha in 850 B.C.

J

JERASH. The ancient Greco-Roman city of Jerash is situated north of Amman. This once prosperous trading town now consists of vast and well-preserved ruins. The most complete and noted architectural remains are the temples of Artemis and Zeus, a large Roman forum, Hadrian's triumphal arch, a functional theater, and a mile-long street of columns.

JERUSALEM. Jerusalem is a holy city for Jews, Christians, and Muslims. In modern history, it served as the British mandatory capital in Palestine. After 1948 the city was divided. The western half became the capital of Israel (q.v.) and the eastern half was in the West Bank (q.v.), which became part of Jordan. King Abdullah was assassinated in the city in 1951. In 1967 Israel captured the city as it took the West Bank. Israel annexed the city shortly thereafter, but no other country in the world has accepted this action as internationally legal. The Palestinians (q.v.) desire to make East Jerusalem the capital of their state when and if they establish a Palestinian state.

JEWS. *See* BALFOUR DECLARATION, ISRAEL.

JOHNSTON PLAN. The Johnston Plan is a scheme for the equitable division of the waters of the Jordan River and its tributaries among its riparian states. It was drawn up in 1954 by Eric Johnston, a hydraulic engineering expert sent by the Eisenhower administration to study the equitable division of the waters of the Jordan River and its tributaries.

JORDAN ARAB ARMY (JAA). The Arab Legion (q.v.) was renamed the Jordan Arab Army in 1956. During this period, the officer corps, which had been led by seconded British officers, was also Arabized. At the time of this writing, the JAA consists of approximately 70,000 officers and enlisted men. (In addition, the air force has a corps of 10,000 men, and the navy has a few hundred.) While the training and standards of the Jordanian military are considered to be high, the quality of its equipment and the number of personnel is considerably below that of its neighbors. Proportionately, the JAA employs about 14% (or 16% for the entire military) of the total manpower. While this may be considered a drain on the economy, the military's contributions to internal and external security are deemed worth the price by the Jordanian regime. *See also* GLUBB.

JORDAN COOPERATIVE ORGANIZATION (JCO). Since the early 1970s, the JCO has overseen the Jordanian cooperative movement. It provides the cooperatives (q.v.) with credit, administrative, technical, and auditing services, and a forum for relations with worldwide cooperative movements.

JORDAN DEVELOPMENT PROGRAM (JDP). The Jordan Development Program for assistance to the West Bank and Gaza was established by Jordan with backing from the United States in 1986. Its purpose was to help to develop these territories and encourage support for Jordan among the Palestinian (q.v.) population living there. The program was canceled in 1988 when Jordan administratively and politically disengaged from the West Bank. *See also* GAZA, WEST BANK.

JORDAN DINAR. The Jordan dinar is the official currency of Jordan.

"JORDAN IS PALESTINE." In the last 10 to 15 years, the phrase "Jordan is Palestine" has become popular among some political circles in Israel (q.v.). The proponents of this view base their statement on two assertions. First, the original British mandate for Palestine (q.v.) included East Jordan (q.v.); second, the majority of East Jordan's population is Palestinian. The political motives for this view are that these circles would like to solve the Palestinian problem in Jordan, not in the West Bank and Gaza or parts of Palestine. With respect to the two key assertions, neither is true. In late 1921 the British High Commissioner for Palestine unilaterally asserted that Transjordan, or East Jordan, came under the Palestine mandate. In the following year, Great Britain submitted papers to the League of Nations stating that Great Britain did not intend to rule East Jordan directly as it did in Palestine and that East Jordan did not fall under the terms of the Balfour Declaration (q.v.). Thus Great Britain drew a distinction and recognized an inherent difference between Palestine and Jordan, or Transjordan, as it was then known. With respect to the latter assertion, statistical data available in the 1980s show that Palestinians (q.v.) make up about 45% of Jordan's population.

JORDAN RIVER. The Jordan River, flowing from the Sea of Galilee to the Dead Sea, divides Jordan from Israel in the northern half of its flow and Jordan from the West Bank in its southern half. According to the Bible, Jesus Christ was baptized in its waters. *See also* DEAD SEA, ISRAEL, WEST BANK.

JORDAN VALLEY. The Jordan Valley is the great rift that runs from close to the Lebanese border through the Sea of Galilee and the Dead Sea and ends in the Wadi al-Araba. The valley is shared by Israel and Syria in the north, Jordan and Israel below the Sea of Galilee, Jordan and the West Bank above the Dead Sea, and Jordan and Israel again below the Dead Sea in the Wadi al-Araba. In Arabic, the Jordan Valley is termed *al-ghor*. The Jordanians have developed the valley extensively. The East Ghor Canal (q.v.), completed in 1964, delivers irrigation water to a complex network that feeds farmers' fields. The Jordan Valley with its irrigation scheme is by far the most productive agricultural area of Jordan. *See also* JORDAN VALLEY AUTHORITY.

JORDAN VALLEY AUTHORITY (JVA). The Jordan Valley Authority, also at times termed the Jordan Valley Development Authority, is in charge of building and administering the development projects in the Jordan Valley. *See also* EAST GHOR CANAL, JORDAN VALLEY.

JORDANIAN-BRITISH TREATIES. *See* ANGLO-JORDANIAN TREATIES.

JORDANIAN-PALESTINIAN JOINT COMMITTEE . The Jordanian-Palestinian Joint Committee, officially known as the Jordanian-Palestinian Committee for the Support of the Steadfastness of the Inhabitants of the Occupied Areas, was set up following the signing of the Camp David Accords (q.v.) in 1978. Funded by the more wealthy Arab states as a result of pledges they made at the 1978 Baghdad Arab summit, the committee administers financial assistance for social and economic development projects and housing loans in the West Bank and Gaza. An equal number of representatives from the Jordanian government and the Palestine Liberation Organization (q.v.) sit on the committee and oversee the funds.

K

KARAK. Karak is a small provincial capital in the west central portion of Jordan. The town has been variously known as Kir of Moab, Kir Haraseth, Petra Deserti, Charac-Moab, Castle of Crac, Pierre du Desert, and al-Karak. The area first appeared in history in 2400 B.C. during the Bronze Age. It enjoyed an advanced sedentary civilization, but this suddenly disappeared in 1800 B.C. About 600 years later, a new civilization, the Moabite Kingdom, developed. It was then that the present-day town of Karak was first settled and fortified. It has been continuously inhabited since that date. Near Karak around the village of Mu'ta, the first battle between the Arab Muslims and the Byzantine Empire was fought. During the Crusader period, Renaud de Châtillon built a magnificent fortress at Karak from which he ruled Jordan. In Mu'ta, one of Jordan's universities was established in the 1980s. Southeast of Karak, next to the Dead Sea, Jordan's potash works were developed in the same decade. The majority of Karak's population is Muslim, but the town and governorate also have a significant Christian minority.

KINSHIP. *See* TRIBES AND KINSHIP.

L

LABOR FORCE. *See* ECONOMY.

LAWRENCE, T. E. (1888–1935). T. E. Lawrence, also known in popular literature as Lawrence of Arabia, was a British officer who assisted the leaders of the Arab Revolt against the Ottoman Empire (q.v.) during World War I. As such he was an adviser to Amir Faisal (q.v.), the military leader of the revolt under his father, Sharif Hussein (q.v.), its political leader. Lawrence later advised Colonial Secretary

Winston Churchill (q.v.) when the mandate for Jordan was being established and Amir Abdullah (q.v.) was accepted as its Arab leader. Lawrence wrote *The Seven Pillars of Wisdom* in which he describes his role in the Arab Revolt.

LEAGUE OF ARAB STATES (LAS). The League of Arab States, also known as the Arab League, is the regional organization of all Arab countries. Jordan was one of its founding members in 1945. The League undertakes cultural, social, educational, agricultural, economic, scientific, security, and political activities.

LEGISLATIVE COUNCIL. The Legislative Council was the Jordanian parliament under the Organic Law of 1928. This body was indirectly elected. It was replaced in the 1946 constitution by a directly elected parliament.

LEVANT. The Levant, a vague geographical term, comprises the countries bordering on the eastern Mediterranean. Some observers include Jordan in the Levant, others do not.

M

MA'AN. Ma'an is a provincial capital in the south of Jordan. A relatively new town, many of the citizens of the Ma'an region are of bedouin (q.v.) origin.

MADABA. Madaba is a provincial capital in the central part of Jordan, south of Amman. An ancient church in the center of town has the oldest map found in Asia. It is mosaic and depicts the eastern Mediterranean region with Jerusalem at its center. For centuries, Madaba had a very small population. It grew considerably in the second half of the nineteenth century when a number of Christians migrated to the area from Karak.

MAMLUKS. In 1260 the Mamluks defeated the Ayyubid dynasty, after which they ruled Jordan and the surrounding region until the arrival of the Ottomans in 1518.

MAQARIN DAM. The Maqarin Dam on the Yarmuk River, a tributary of the Jordan River, has been planned for decades. When completed, an additional 35,000 acres will be brought under cultivation in the Jordan Valley as the lake behind the dam feeds the East Ghor Canal. The building of the dam was held up until 1987 by the sensitive issue of riparian rights among Jordan, Syria, Israel, and the West Bank. Syria and Jordan resolved the issues via direct negotiations; through the good offices of the United States, Israel and Jordan were able to reach an understanding on mutual water rights. Preliminary work on the dam was started soon thereafter, but stalled again in 1990. Syria and Jordan have renamed the Maqarin Dam al-Wahda, or the Unity Dam. *See also* EAST GHOR CANAL, JOHNSTON PLAN, JORDAN RIVER, JORDAN VALLEY.

MILITARY. *See* ARAB LEGION, JORDAN ARAB ARMY.

MILLET. During Ottoman times a millet was a non-Muslim religious minority group that was officially recognized by the Ottoman Empire (q.v.) and given certain autonomous rights. These rights involved rules and regulations and their application with respect to the group's internal religious affairs, personal-status law, and commercial relations, so long as these pertained only to members of the group.

MINORITIES. *See* ARMENIANS, CHRISTIANS, CIRCAS-SIANS, PALESTINIANS, SHISHANIS.

MOAB. The geographical area of Moab is approximately the area of modern Madaba, Karak, and Tafila. The Israelites conquered the region ca. 950 B.C. In 850 B.C. King Mesha reestablished Moabite control in the region. The Nabatean Arabs established their presence in the region ca. 500 B.C.

MOUNT NEBO. Southeast of Amman is Mount Nebo, from which the Jordan Valley, the Dead Sea, and the holy city of Jerusalem may be seen. A number of intricate mosaics are located in ancient Byzantine churches on and near the mount.

MUKHTAR. A mukhtar is a village official who is elected by the village families and is confirmed by the central government. His is an ambiguous position, for he is at once at the service of his family, tribe, and village, but also of the government. Given this ambiguity, at times his obligations may conflict. The duties of the office include authenticating numerous official papers on behalf of the people, recording births and deaths, keeping record of where people live, accompanying the police on any official business, and being a liaison with government programs in the village.

MUNICIPAL COUNCIL. *See* MUNICIPALITY.

MUNICIPALITY. In the 1890s the Ottoman Empire (q.v.) introduced the municipality law to Jordan. Under the law, many provincial towns formed institutional structures composed of an elected municipal council and an executive headed by the president of the council, or the mayor as he is called in the West. Initially these institutions did not work well in Jordan because they were essentially an alien import imposed on a traditional society. Over time they have developed, however; by the 1970s most observers believed they were fulfilling their functions.

MUSLIM. *See* ISLAM.

MUSLIM BROTHERHOOD. The Muslim Brotherhood, a political party and social service organization, has for decades been the only legal political group in Jordan. King Hussein (q.v.) allowed this fundamentalist religious party to be active because of its support for him and its role as a safety valve for fervent Muslims. The party consistently sided with the king during the troubled times of the 1950s, 1967, and 1970. In the 1950s the brotherhood won seats in parliament (q.v.). In the by-elections of 1984, it again won a number of seats, but not in its own name. In the early 1980s the Muslim Brotherhood used Jordan as a base for violent activities in Syria (q.v.). As Jordan attempted to improve its relations with Syria after 1985, the government severely curtailed the organization's activities. Finally, candidates associated with the brotherhood were quite successful in the 1989 parliamentary elections. *See also* ISLAM.

N

NABATEAN. The Nabateans (or Nabataeans), an Arabic-speaking group famous for trade, established itself in Jordan in the fifth century B.C. They ruled from their unique capital carved out of the rose-colored cliffs of Petra. Their architecture was strongly influenced by the Greeks, Ptolemies, and Romans.

NASSER, GAMEL ABDEL (1918–1970). President of Egypt from the early 1950s to 1970, Nasser was the most prominent, charismatic, and powerful Arab leader of his time. His advocacy of Arab nationalism and his ability to speak directly to the Arab people shook conservative Arab regimes on many occasions, including Jordan in the 1950s and 1960s. Nasser led the Arab countries into the 1967 war with Israel (q.v.), whereby Jordan lost the West Bank (q.v.) to Israeli military occupation. Only in the last couple of years of Nasser's presidency were he and King Hussein (q.v.) close. *See also* ARAB NATIONALISM, EGYPT.

NATIONAL ASSEMBLY. The National Assembly is made up of the Chamber of Deputies, which is elected by the Jordanian people, and the Senate, which is appointed by the king. *See also* GOVERNMENT, PARLIAMENT.

NATIONAL CHARTER. Following the nationwide 1989 parliamentary elections in Jordan, King Hussein ibn Talal (q.v.) in April 1990 appointed a royal commission of 60 noted people to write a national charter to define the parameters of and develop a consensus on the terms for Jordanian political life. The commission brought together all shades of political opinion, including Arab nationalists, the Muslim Brotherhood (q.v.) and independent Islamicists, communists and other leftists, technocrats, centrists, and traditional tribal leaders. In December, the commission completed and endorsed the charter, which stresses democracy and pluralism and allows for the formation of Jordanian-financed and -based political parties (as opposed to the older Arab national and Islamic parties, which straddled borders). In June 1991, a national conference of 2,000 leaders endorsed the National Charter and the king signed it.

NATIONAL CONSULTATIVE COUNCIL (NCC). The National Consultative Council, appointed by the king, sat from 1978 to 1983 during a period when parliament (q.v.) was dissolved. By gentlemen's agreement the cabinet issued no laws that were not debated and approved by this council.

NATIONAL PLANNING COUNCIL (NPC). Established in the early 1970s, the National Planning Council was the primary agency responsible for social and economic planning in Jordan until it was replaced by the Ministry of

Planning in the late 1980s. Crown Prince Hassan (q.v.), who is very instrumental in Jordan's development (q.v.) process, was chairman of the National Planning Council. *See also* ECONOMY.

NATIONAL SOCIALIST PARTY. The National Socialist Party, led by Sulayman Nabulsi, was an active radical Arab nationalist party in the 1950s. Unlike the other significant political parties active in Jordan, this party did not have branches in other Arab countries. In the 1956 elections, it won a plurality of the seats in the Chamber of Deputies (parliament). Accordingly, its leader, Sulayman Nabulsi, was asked to form a government. This government lasted only until 1957, when it was dismissed after Sulayman Nabulsi and army commander General Ali Abu Nuwar led an aborted coup d'etat. By the 1960s the party had disappeared.

NESTORIANS. *See* ASSYRIANS.

O

ORGANIC LAW. The Organic Law, Jordan's first "constitution," was promulgated in 1928, the same year the first Anglo-Jordanian Treaty (q.v.) was signed.

OTTOMAN EMPIRE. The Ottoman Empire, originally based in Asia Minor and southern Europe, conquered the Arab Middle East, including Jordan, in 1518. For the greater period of Ottoman presence in Jordan, which endured for 400 years until 1918, little direct control was exercised. Rather, from their provincial capital in Damascus, the Ottoman authorities occasionally sent armed patrols to the region, collected meager taxes, and paid bedouin (q.v.) tribes to protect (or not raid) the pilgrimage route to Mecca. Actual local control was in the hands of settled and nomadic or bedouin tribes. This pattern did not obtain in the first half-century after the Ottoman conquest, when the officials and military maintained an actual presence and direct rule, or in the period after 1870, when the Ottomans started to reassert direct control in the northern part of Jordan. At this time the Ottomans encouraged the Circassians (q.v.) to settle in Jordan, partly to help contain the bedouin. During World War I, the Hashemites (q.v.) led the great Arab Revolt against the Ottoman Empire with the help of the British. In 1917–1918, the British and the Arabs drove the Ottomans out of Jordan, Palestine, Lebanon, and Syria as the Ottoman Empire was in the last stages of its collapse.

Some authors refer to the Ottomans as the Ottoman Turks or just the Turks. Because the Ottoman Empire was composed not only of Turks, but also Arabs, other Middle Eastern ethnic groups, and Europeans, serious scholars employ the term *Ottoman* or *Ottoman Empire*.

P

PALESTINE. The land of Palestine lies to the west of the Jordan River and the Wadi al-Araba. It is claimed by both the Israelis and the Palestinian Arabs: two peoples claim one land as their homeland—the primary source of the Arab-Israeli conflict (q.v.). In biblical times, the Canaanites, the Philistines, and the Israelites, along with other peoples, lived in and ruled Palestine. From the time of Alexander the Great, Palestine was conquered and ruled in a similar pattern to that of Jordan. The Ottoman Empire (q.v.) lost control of Palestine to the British at the end of World War I. During that war, Great Britain (q.v.) issued the Balfour Declaration (q.v.), declaring Palestine to be the homeland for the Jews. During the British mandate from 1918 to 1948, Palestine was subject to considerable migration of European Jews, who soon came into conflict with the indigenous Palestinian Arabs who lived there. In 1948 the State of Israel was set up in part of Palestine. In southwestern Palestine, the Gaza Strip, into which hundreds of thousands of Palestinian refugees had fled, was administered by Egypt. The West Bank, where hundreds of thousands of Palestinian refugees also fled, was occupied by the Arab Legion in 1948 and was united with the East Bank in the Hashemite Kingdom of Jordan in 1950. Other Palestinian refugees fled to Lebanon and Syria. In 1967 the whole of the land of Palestine came under Israeli control as the Israeli military captured the Gaza Strip and the West Bank from Egypt and Jordan, respectively. As of this writing, both territories remain under Israeli military occupation. Many Israelis refer to Palestine as *Eretz Israel,* which in Hebrew means land of Israel. *See also* GAZA, ISRAEL, WEST BANK.

PALESTINE LIBERATION ORGANIZATION (PLO). The Palestine Liberation Organization was created by the Rabat Arab summit of 1964. Its first chairman was Ahmad Shukairy, a fiery orator, and the organization originally followed Egyptian political direction. In 1969 Palestinian guerrilla groups gained control of the PLO, and the leader of one of them, Fatah's Yasser Arafat, became the chairman of the PLO. The PLO was heavily involved in the Jordanian civil war of 1970. In the 1980s King Hussein and Chairman Arafat's relations were frequently estranged, but occasionally they coordinated their policies toward Israel. In 1988 King Hussein's disengagement from the West Bank left the negotiating field to the PLO. *See also* ARAB-ISRAELI CONFLICT, ARAFAT, FATAH, PALESTINE NATIONAL COUNCIL, PALESTINIANS, POPULAR FRONT FOR THE LIBERATION OF PALESTINE, WEST BANK.

PALESTINE NATIONAL COUNCIL (PNC). The Palestine National Council is the parliament in exile of the Palestini-

ans. The Palestine Liberation Organization (q.v.) answers
to it. Its members are elected by popular organizations,
such as labor unions, selected by guerrilla groups, and
appointed from among Palestinian notables.

PALESTINIANS. Palestinians are the Arabs who originate
from Palestine (q.v.). About half of all Palestinians live
under Israeli rule. Over half a million live in Israel (q.v.),
and the same number are in the Gaza Strip. About one
million live in the West Bank (q.v.), including Arab East
Jerusalem. In Jordan (that is, the East Bank [q.v.]), about
45% of the population is Palestinian. (Until recently, con-
ventional wisdom said that the Palestinian population of
the East Bank was between 55% and 70%. However, the
census of 1979 and recent scholarship indicate that the
percentage is much less—about 45%.) A few hundred
thousand each live in Lebanon, Syria, and until fall 1990,
Kuwait.

The difference between the Palestinians and the people
who originate from east of the Jordan River, or East Jordanians for our purposes here, constitutes the most serious
division in Jordan. Prior to 1948 the problem did not exist:
there were only East Jordanians in Jordan, which at that
time consisted only of the land east of the Jordan River and
the Wadi al-Araba. One of the major consequences of the
1948–1949 Arab-Israeli war was the incorporation of the
West Bank into Jordan and the conferring of Jordanian
citizenship on the Palestinians of the West Bank and the
Palestinian refugees who had fled from Israel to the West
and East Banks. While it is impossible to categorize all
Palestinians the same way, it can be said that historically
the Jordanian Palestinians had fundamentally different
national aims from those of the East Jordanians. The latter
focus on the East Bank, its institutions, and the process of
development. While most would like to see the West Bank
and Gaza Strip relieved of Israeli military occupation, this
is not their top priority. On the other hand, for many of the

Jordanian Palestinians, their primary national priority is to free part—or for some, all—of the land of Palestine from Israeli control and establish a Palestinian state. Thus these Palestinians see Jordanian citizenship as a convenience rather than an identity or a loyalty.

By 1989 these views and national outlooks have evolved. A portion, perhaps a significant portion, still have the same national outlook described above. However, it can clearly be stated that a significant portion do not; rather they have become Jordanian in outlook. They do not deny their Palestinian origins, indeed they are proud of them. They would like to see the West Bank and Gaza freed of military occupation. But their primary focus is on Jordan, its problems and prospects.

The road from one orientation to another has not always been smooth. Intensive relations between Jordan and the Palestinians start with the events of 1948–1949. Jordan acquired Palestinian territory with the agreement of Great Britain and, it is reported, with the secret approval of the Zionists. In 1950 the West Bank was joined with Jordan in the Hashemite Kingdom of Jordan by a vote of a parliament elected from the East and West Banks. During the 1950s the Palestinian refugees, found primarily in the West Bank but also in the East Bank, were trying to put their lives back together. For the most part they were politically quiet. Some would occasionally make trips into Israel to see their lost lands, to retrieve possessions from the homes they had fled, or to exact revenge. These actions would stimulate harsh military responses from Israel. Jordan attempted to control the Palestinians' movement in order to avoid this tension, but the regime was not always successful. The nonrefugee Palestinians of the West Bank had a different relationship to Amman. Most just acquiesced to a new ruler, this time a Jordanian Arab ruler. Some of the elite in the big towns actively joined in Jordanian politics, became part of the system, and benefited considerably. Other elites, for nationalistic or ideological reasons, were active politically in opposition to Amman. Most often members of this latter group joined the radical Arab nationalist parties, which were opposed to the Hashemites (q.v.).

The 1960s partially continued the pattern of the 1950s, but new and powerful elements were added that came to dominate Palestinian politics by the end of the decade. Many of the rural people in the West Bank remained quiescent and accepted Hashemite rule from Amman. Some urban elites also continued to participate in and benefit from the system. However, in the early 1960s other Palestinians, largely outside of Jordan, started founding the guerrilla movements. They decided to take this initiative because they judged that both the old Palestinian politicians and the Arab nationalist parties were not going to be able to liberate Palestine. Also, in 1964 the Rabat Arab summit founded the Palestine Liberation Organization (q.v.), which, along with the guerrilla groups, would challenge Jordan's existence. These actions, in conjunction with other Arab and Israeli actions, led to the 1967 Arab-Israeli war during which Jordan lost the West Bank to Israeli military occupation. An immediate consequence of this loss was a new wave of Palestinian refugees. About 300,000 refugees, many from the camps strung along the west side of the Jordan Valley, fled for a second time in their lives, this time to the East Bank. Within a few months another 30,000–50,000 Gaza Palestinians were forced or persuaded to cross the river into Jordan. Another outcome of the war was an immense growth in the popularity of the Palestinian guerrilla movements and a rapid growth of their presence in Jordan. In the late 1960s King Hussein (q.v.) even made a speech in which he said that someday all people of Jordan may be guerrillas. However, the relations between the Amman government and the Palestinian guerrilla groups deteriorated by the summer of 1970 into a civil war that reached its culmination in September. King Hussein and the Jordan Arab Army prevailed, but at the cost of considerable loss of life. Importantly, though, the majority of the Palestinians of Jordan stayed out of the fighting. Indeed, 50% of the army was Palestinian, and the vast majority of them remained loyal to the king.

During the 1970s, the relations between the Palestinians and Amman took two very different routes. The Palestinians who identified with the guerrilla groups and the PLO became more estranged, while those who elected to throw their lot with Jordan continued to benefit in employment and in prosperity. Security problems arising from the Palestinian guerrilla groups were endemic in the first half of the decade. Jordan frequently suffered from their actions and had to maintain constant vigilance. Diplomatically, Jordan also suffered. In 1974 the Arab summit at Rabat passed a resolution declaring the PLO to be the sole legitimate representative of the Palestinian people. This action bolstered the reputation of the PLO, Yasser Arafat, and the Palestinians. It served to undermine King Hussein's relations with the Palestinians, especially his claim to the West Bank. Nevertheless, Amman retained a significant role there. The West Bank Palestinians still enjoyed Jordanian citizenship. Jordan still paid the salaries of its West Bank employees, who numbered over 10,000. It provided economic assistance to such West Bank Palestinian organizations as charities, municipalities (q.v.), and agricultural and housing cooperatives (q.v.). In addition, the bridges over the Jordan River (q.v.) remained open for commerce and personal, professional, and tourist travel. Last, as noted elsewhere in this dictionary, Jordan experienced considerable economic growth starting in 1975. Most of the Palestinians of the East Bank benefited from this, as well as from the relatively high level of personal freedom accorded all Jordanians. The Palestinians of the East Bank were in a good position to benefit from this growth because in the 1970s, as a group, they still enjoyed somewhat higher educational standards than their counterparts whose forefathers came from the East Bank. Except for a short period

in the mid-1970s following the Rabat Arab summit decision, the Palestinians continued to hold a proportional
share of cabinet posts and other high-level positions. Their
numbers dropped in the military for a time, but grew again
and reached ordinary levels by the late 1970s.

The pattern of the late 1970s partially held in the 1980s.
Those Palestinians who identified with Jordan were normal participants in the Jordanian experience. The Palestinian guerrilla groups, however, by the late 1970s had
largely shifted their focus from Jordan to Israel. Also,
especially after the PLO was partially driven out of Lebanon by the Israeli invasion of 1982, Yasser Arafat started
off-and-on negotiations with King Hussein. In 1984 the
Palestine National Council (q.v.) held a full session in
Amman. Following this historic event, in 1985 Hussein and
Arafat worked out accords for a framework for peace with
Israel, but these were abandoned in 1987. After a brief
period during which King Hussein attempted to attract
direct support from Palestinians in the West Bank, he
decided to alter fundamentally Jordan's relations with the
West Bank and thus the terms of the Arab-Israeli conflict.
This decision was taken largely in reaction to the Palestinian uprising, or *intifada* (q.v.), by which the Palestinians
were expressing their disdain for Jordan and their adher-
ence to Palestinian nationalism. Thus, in the summer of
1988 King Hussein announced Jordan's political and administrative disengagement from the West Bank. By this
action, he was turning the field over to the PLO and
focusing diplomatic attention on the need to solve the
Arab-Israeli conflict between the two key parties: Israel
and the Palestinians. That a Jordanian-Palestinian confederation might play a role in an eventual peace resolution,
though, was not denied by King Hussein's actions. Last,
despite the disengagement, Jordan did not take the step of
relinquishing its claim to sovereignty over the West Bank,
nor did it withdraw Jordanian citizenship from the residents of the West Bank, although their rights were limited.

See also ARAB-ISRAELI CONFLICT, ARAFAT, BLACK SEPTEMBER.

PARLIAMENT. Jordan's first parliament, called the Legislative Council, was elected indirectly in 1928 under the then prevailing constitution, the Organic Law. Under the new constitution promulgated in 1946, the parliament was directly elected and officially termed the Chamber of Deputies. The upper house, appointed by the king, is the Senate. The parliament elected in 1967 sat until 1974, was dissolved, but recalled in 1976 and again dismissed in that year. In 1984 parliament was once again recalled, and by-elections were held in that year and in 1986. The king dissolved parliament in the summer of 1988. In November 1989 nationwide parliamentary elections were held and shortly thereafter parliament began holding periodic sessions. *See also* GOVERNMENT.

PEAKE, COLONEL F. G. (1886–1970). In 1921, in the early days of the Amirate of Jordan (Transjordan), Major Peake, a British officer, founded the Arab reserve force that was reorganized and renamed the Arab Legion in 1923. He headed this Jordanian armed force until he was replaced by Colonel Glubb in 1939. *See also* ARAB LEGION, GLUBB.

PEASANT. *See* FELLAH.

PERSIAN GULF CRISIS AND WAR. In August 1990 Iraq invaded and occupied Kuwait. The consequences of this action for Jordan were manyfold. First, Jordan strongly condemned the Iraqi military invasion and occupation of Kuwait, but it also questioned the subsequent introduction of non-Arab, non-Muslim troops into Saudi Arabia. This latter attitude strained its relations with the United States (which led the coalition against Iraqi actions) and Saudi Arabia (which had invited the U.S. and coalition troops).

Second, the crisis precipitated a massive exit of third country nations—primarily Egyptians and South Asians—from Kuwait and to a lesser extent Iraq. Over 900,000 evacuees crossed the border into Jordan. That country, with considerable international assistance, then organized a massive effort to repatriate them. Third, about 240,000 Jordanians, largely of Palestinian origin, also fled Kuwait, took up residence in Jordan, and thereby increased the country's population by 7%. Fourth, the crisis caused a major economic downturn, virtually doubling unemployment. Fifth, Jordan did not join the U.S.-led war of early 1991 against Iraq, but its population feared that the war would spread to Jordan, a fear that fortunately for the country was not realized. Sixth, Jordan's relations with the conservative Arab states of the Arabian Peninsula—Saudi Arabia, Kuwait, United Arab Emirates—continued to be strained after the war. However, Jordan and the U.S. at least partially reconciled and Jordan was again central to the spring and summer 1991 U.S.-sponsored peace initiative to resolve the Arab-Israeli and Palestinian-Israeli conflicts.

PETRA. Petra, the ancient capital of the Nabateans (q.v.), is in southern Jordan close to the Wadi al-Araba. This unique city, hidden in the encircling craggy rock mountains south of the Dead Sea (q.v.), is mostly carved in the rose-colored cliff faces of a deep valley. The only easy access is through the *siq* or a narrow defile flanked by towering cliffs. At the end of the siq is the *khazneh* or treasury, a dramatic vista visible only after traversing the narrow defile for a kilometer. Found within the valley are intricate buildings and edifices hewn from live rock. In addition to the numerous small and large houses, one also discovers a gigantic *dair* or monastery, the palace tomb, and an amphitheater in Greco-Roman style.

PHOSPHATE. Phosphate, a component of agricultural fertilizer, is Jordan's major extractive industry and export. Phosphate mines were opened in the 1960s and expanded in the 1970s and 1980s. In the last decade, Jordan has also established large phosphate processing facilities that make fertilizer.

POLITICAL PARTIES. Generally, political parties have always been illegal in Jordan. The one major exception is the Muslim Brotherhood, a political party and social organization that the regime has allowed to operate openly. Nevertheless, parties have been active in the country, mostly in the 1950s and 1960s, but some have maintained activities until the time of this writing. The National Charter (q.v.), adopted by a national conference and signed by the king in June 1991, states that Jordanian-financed and -based political parties are to be permitted in future Jordanian political life. *See also* BA'TH PARTY, COMMUNIST PARTY, ISLAMIC PARTY OF LIBERATION, MUSLIM BROTHERHOOD, NATIONAL SOCIALIST PARTY.

POPULAR FRONT FOR THE LIBERATION OF PALESTINE (PFLP). The PFLP is one of the more radical of the Palestinian guerrilla organizations. Some of its founders had been active with the Arab Nationalist Movement, a radical nationalist pan-Arab party. George Habash has been the leader of the PFLP for most of its existence. At the time of the 1970 fighting in Jordan, the PFLP took a leadership role in stimulating the conflict, including hijacking commercial aircraft and requiring them to land at an abandoned Jordanian desert airfield. Unlike Fatah, during the strife, it called for the elimination of Hashemite rule. *See also* BLACK SEPTEMBER, PALESTINE LIBERATION ORGANIZATION, PALESTINIANS.

POTASH. Potash, an important component of agricultural fertilizer, is extracted by Jordan from the mineral-rich waters of the Dead Sea (q.v.). This industry, which was established in the 1980s, is oriented toward exportation.

PRIME MINISTER. The prime minister is appointed by the king. The prime minister and the council of ministers (cabinet) that he heads are responsible to the chamber of deputies, or parliament. A list of noted prime ministers throughout the history of Jordan would include Tawfiq Abul-Huda (1930s–1950s), Samir Rifai (1930s–1960s), Ibrahim Hashim (1930s--1950s), Sulayman Nabulsi (1950s), Haza' al-Majali (1950s–1960s), Wasfi al-Tal (1960s–1970s), Said Mufti (1950s–1960s), Zaid Rifai (1970s–1980s), Mudar Badran (1970s–1980s), Ahmad Obeidat (1980s), Sharif Abdul Hamid Sharaf (1960s–1970s, 1979–1980), Zaid bin Shaker (1980s) and Tahir al-Masri (1991–   ). *See also* GOVERNMENT.

PTOLEMY. The Ptolemies, successors to Alexander the Great, ruled Jordan from 322 B.C. until the Romans gained control ca. 70–60 B.C.

R

RAILROAD. *See* HEJAZ RAILROAD.

REAGAN MIDDLE EAST PEACE PLAN. The Reagan Middle East Peace Plan, a major initiative of President Ronald Reagan's administration, was presented to the public on September 1, 1982. Like previous U.S. initiatives, it was based on United Nations Resolution 242 (q.v.), whereby land is to be exchanged for peace. Following the partially successful Camp David Accords (q.v.), it was based on the principles of that agreement as well. While leaving the ultimate disposition of the West Bank and Gaza to negotiations among the involved parties, the Reagan Plan did envision an Arab Jordanian future for the West

Bank and Gaza, not an Israeli future. The United States did not follow up this initiative with any significant diplomatic activity.

REFUGEES. The only refugees of any significance in Jordan are those from Palestine. They came to the West and East Banks during and following the 1948–1949 Arab-Israeli war. The 1967 war produced a new wave of refugees. They came to the East Bank mostly from refugee camps in the West Bank, but some also came from Gaza. *See also* PALESTINE, PALESTINIANS, UNITED NATIONS RELIEF AND WORKS AGENCY FOR PALESTINE REFUGEES.

RELIGION. *See* CHRISTIANS, ISLAM.

ROMANS. The Romans conquered Jordan ca. 70–60 B.C. and ruled until they were replaced by the Byzantines in the fourth and fifth centuries A.D. The Romans left many archaeological ruins in Jordan, including the magnificent trading city of Jerash and major sights in Amman, which had been called Philadelphia in the Roman era.

ROYAL COURT. The royal court administers the palace and advises the king. The king appoints officers of the royal court, and they serve at his pleasure. Serving in the royal court has frequently been a stepping stone to higher office in Jordan.

ROYAL SCIENTIFIC SOCIETY (RSS). The Royal Scientific Society is a major research institution of Jordan. Chaired by Crown Prince Hassan (q.v.), it conducts economic, social, electronic, agricultural, engineering, and scientific research. Its orientation is to undertake applied studies that have an immediate practical application.

S

SALADIN (1138–1193). Known in Arabic as Salah al-Din, Saladin was the Muslim leader who defeated the Crusaders and drove them out of Jerusalem. In 1187 he also defeated the Crusaders at Karak (q.v.), after which Muslim rule returned to Jordan. His rule initiated the Ayyubid dynasty. *See also* CRUSADERS.

SALT. Salt is a small provincial capital west of Amman and north of the Dead Sea. An old Jordanian town, it has a Muslim majority and a Christian minority. Its economy traditionally has been focused on agriculture and agricultural services.

SAUDI ARABIA. Saudi Arabia is Jordan's southern and eastern neighbor. In the early years of Jordan, relations were marked by hostility, but these have given way to often close working relations based on mutual national interests. In 1922 and again in 1924, Saudi Arabia invaded Jordan as it was piecing together its own state in Arabia. A number of the battles in that pursuit were against Hashemite (q.v.) rule in Mecca, which it eventually defeated. Presumably Saudi Arabia was attacking Jordan, then ruled by a Hashemite, Amir Abdullah (q.v.), in the same vein it was attacking his father or brother in Mecca. Since the mid-1920s, however, the border has been quiet. In the mid-1960s, Saudi Arabia and Jordan exchanged territory along Jordan's southern border so that Jordan could expand its only port of Aqaba. In the last three decades, the two countries, both conservative monarchies, have recognized that they enjoy mutual interests and have usually adopted complementary policies with respect to Arab and Muslim issues. Jordan has also received financial assistance from oil-rich Saudi Arabia.

SELJUKS. The Seljuk Turks replaced the Abbasids as rulers of the Muslim Middle East in 1071. Shortly thereafter, they lost control of the Levant to the Crusaders.

SENATE. The Senate, or Council of Notables, appointed by the king, is the upper house of Jordan's National Assembly. *See also* GOVERNMENT.

SHARIA. The sharia is Muslim religious law. In Jordan, religious law is applied in religious courts but restricted to matters of personal status, such as marriage, divorce, inheritance, orphans, and child custody.

SHARIF. In Arabic, sharif is the title for descendants of the Prophet Muhammad.

SHAYKH. A shaykh, also spelled *sheik* or *sheikh,* is an Arab leader. In Jordan the term is usually associated with a tribal leader or a religious leader. The term also denotes respect and honor, and usually, but not always, a shaykh is an older man.

SHISHANI. The Shishanis are a small ethnic Muslim minority group that originate from the Caucasus in the present-day Soviet Union. They came to Jordan at the urging of the Ottomans during the 1880s.

SUMMITS. *See* ARAB SUMMITS.

SUNNI. Sunni Islam is Orthodox Islam as opposed to Shia Islam. The Muslims of Jordan are virtually all Sunni. *See also* ISLAM.

SYRIA. Syria is Jordan's northern neighbor. Except for brief periods, Jordanian-Syrian relations have always been strained. Before World War II, Arab politicians in the French mandate of Syria were generally quite critical of

Amir Abdullah (q.v.), especially for his Hashemite (q.v.) Greater Syria (q.v.) ideas. After World War II, many of the politicians of independent Syria viewed themselves as the guardians of Arab nationalism (q.v.), and some adhered to the radical branch of Arab nationalism. Thus in rhetoric and occasionally deed they were the opponents of Hashemite Jordan. In 1958 Syria united with Egypt (q.v.). The United Arab Republic (UAR), as the two countries were then called, often challenged Jordan. After the break-up of the UAR in 1961, the radical Arab nationalist Ba'th Party (q.v.) gained control of Syria. Except for a brief period in the mid-1970s, Jordanian-Syrian relations have been continually and often severely strained during Ba'th rule. The underlying reasons are the two countries' conflicting views of Arab nationalism, different ideological outlooks with respect to capitalism and socialism, and Syria's ambitions in the Middle East. In 1970 Syria briefly invaded Jordan during Jordan's civil war with the Palestinians, and in 1981 it drew up troops along the Jordanian border. In the early 1980s the Muslim Brotherhood (q.v.) used Jordan as a base for violent activities in Syria. After 1985 Jordan reined in the Muslim Brotherhood and attempted to improve relations with Syria. Throughout the 1980s, Jordan strongly supported Iraq, Syria's archenemy, in its war with Iran, while Syria was on the side of Iran. *See also* ASSAD.

T

TAFILA. Tafila is a small provincial capital in the southern portion of Jordan. Its tribes have had traditionally close relations with Karak (q.v.), and it was at one time part of the same governorate.

TALAL IBN ABDULLAH, KING. Talal, son of King Abdullah of Jordan, was born in 1909 in Mecca. He acceded to the throne upon his father's assassination in 1951. Suffering from severe schizophrenia, he was constitutionally removed from office in 1952. He spent his remaining years until his death in 1972 in a Turkish nursing home. He had three sons: Hussein, Muhammad, and Hassan. *See also* ABDULLAH IBN HUSSEIN, HASSAN IBN TALAL, HUSSEIN IBN TALAL.

TRANSJORDAN. Transjordan, also written *Trans-Jordan* and *TransJordan,* was the common name for East Jordan or the East Bank (q.v.) before World War II.

TRANSJORDAN FRONTIER FORCE (TFF). During the early 1920s, bedouin raiding was an endemic problem in Jordan. Internally in Jordan, the problem was addressed by the Arab Legion (q.v.). To address the external, or cross-border, problem of raiding, the British created the Transjordan Frontier Force in 1926. Recruited primarily from Palestine, its units patrolled and guarded the Jordanian and Palestinian frontiers. *See also* GREAT BRITAIN.

TRIBES AND KINSHIP. Tribes are important sociopolitical groups in Jordan. Both nomadic and settled Jordanians organize themselves into tribes. Thus many of the fellahs (q.v.), or peasants, are members of tribes as are the bedouin. Looking at tribes from another perspective, Jordanians so organized have traditionally exhibited considerable loyalty to the Hashemites (q.v.). As Jordan modernizes and the people enjoy higher levels of education and greater job mobility, the nature of this tribal loyalty to the throne has evolved. Basically, these Jordanians have moved from the position whereby they would give the king virtually total executive freedom to the position whereby they think they should have a role in the political process, some level of authority and responsibility for decision making and execution.

What is the Jordanian tribe and the kinship inherent within it? As noted, it is one of the most important sociopolitical groups in the country. Structurally, it may be described as a corporate territorial group with pyramidal and segmentary qualities. The tribes of Jordan, though, differ considerably in relative size, geographical location, mode of livelihood, and degree of political power.

Kinship and marriage patterns are an integral part of the Jordan tribal systems. Although the tribe is definitely not a kin group but a territorial one, kin groups are basic parts of it, blending into its structure in such a way that it is difficult to distinguish where the kin group ends and the tribal structure begins. In addition, the local tradition of each Jordanian tribe often holds that all its members, or all the members of one section, are descended from one man. In actuality, a subgroup of four to six generations is the only true, coherent kin group. But the tradition is useful for sociopolitical purposes, for it tends to bind people more closely together.

The Jordanians, like most Arabs, reckon kinship through the male line. Politically, this patrilineal pattern is significant, because it tends to create neat, segregated units and subunits within a tribe. A man's identity is more strongly attached to this group than to any other; the behavior of an individual is considered to be the extension of that of his kin, and, conversely, the actions of a man's blood relatives heavily reflect upon him. The kin unit is further reinforced by the marriage preference for one's parallel cousin (father's brother's daughter). If no first cousin on the paternal side is available, then two other preferences become operative. Paternal cousins of a lesser degree are frequently chosen, and a cross-cousin (mother's brother's daughter or father's sister's daughter) is also sought. Quite often in Jordan, because of the general marriage pattern, a cross-cousin is a paternal cousin as well, only of a more distant relationship. This marriage pattern then creates a web of both kin and conjugal ties within a relatively small unit, binding its members together. Thus all the children in the male line of a man who lived four to six generations previous may be considered as a corporate group with a common identity and some joint sociopolitical functions.

The structure of a tribe may have infinite variations, but all within a basic pyramidal pattern. The significance of this pyramidal pattern is that there is an overall vertical organization of the tribe, not just a series of horizontal units with the same identity. But the Jordanian tribe is also inherently segmentary: each segment at each level has a separate identity and a degree of power and authority of its own. Coupling the two concepts—pyramidal and segmentary—together indicates that the tribe is organized in an ascending series of segments, each being a sociopolitical group at some time and in some events. Thus each unit at a structurally higher level automatically contains all the groups below it. Nor does any real leadership hierarchy connect the groups; instead, for example, the shaykh (q.v.) of one of the subsections is in turn the shaykh of the section of which it is a part; similarly, the shaykh of one of the sections is shaykh of the tribe.

Aside from being a pyramidal group, the tribe is also an actively segmenting group. This process, which takes a period of time—perhaps a generation or more—means that a given group undergoes a division, but that the group remains a social entity. In this way a new extended family is created if a man has male offspring and they in turn have male children. A new sublineage or lineage may be formed by the addition of a generation or two within this pattern. This pattern continues at higher levels of the tribal pyramid as well. The occasion for the formation of new major sections of a tribe may stem from the recognition of separate identity due to the activity of this group, or through the setting up of a separate living area (a new village or encampment).

Equally important in this process is the way Jordanians acknowledge their kin relationships. They generally trace four or five generations quite accurately with little or no disagreement among themselves. But, by the fifth or sixth generation the reckoning becomes blurred, showing a definite lack of agreement as to what the true kin relationships are. This blurring usually exists among those who claim a direct relationship with the man who is supposedly the father of all those of a lineage. Structurally, then, it is easy to break off—segment off—a new group at this level and, conversely, to "forget" a generation or more, bringing all into a closer, though fictitious, relationship. Occasionally, an outsider and his family may wish to join a tribe, and it is at this subsection level that he is most easily grafted onto the structure because of its only quasi-kinship nature. If a much larger group is to join a tribe, it usually does so as a larger unit at a higher level in the pyramidal structure— that is, a section. Marriage customs are favorable to all these processes, for they tend to reinforce a small, inward-looking group, commonly not above the sublineage level, as described above. Intermarriage between major sections of a tribe is not common. Thus if a new group is grafted onto a tribe, its position in terms of kin and marriage relationships is not unlike the already existing relations between the various original sections. This is especially true if the newly added section has been resident in the tribal area, for a few mutual marriages will have been contracted during that period.

Apart from segmenting, the phenomenon of fission may occur—that is, a section of a tribe may split off to form a separate one, distinct in identity and organization. Or a section may segment off, settle in a different region in Jordan, and eventually become known as a separate tribe.

As to residence, traditionally a tribal section tends to reside wholly in one encampment or village, or even a quarter of the village. A larger tribe may have sections in a few encampments or villages, while a smaller tribe will naturally be in fewer geographical locations. With the advent of greater Jordanian mobility in the last couple of generations, these residential patterns have started to blur, especially as rural people move to the cities.

The distribution of wealth and material goods within a tribe varies considerably. If the tribe is small and poor, there is very little material difference among its members. If it is large, some of its members, sections, or lineages will be richer than others and usually more powerful. Although common economic activity (such as communal farming) above the extended-family level is not at all common, more wealthy members of a tribe frequently provide services for poorer tribe members.

In Arabic, the settled fellah tribe is known as an *'ashira* in Jordan, while the bedouin tribe is a *qabila*.

U

'ULAMA. The *'ulama* are the religiously learned men of Islam. In Jordan, many are supported by the Ministry of Awqaf, Islamic Affairs, and Holy Places. *See also* ISLAM.

UMAYYADS. The Muslim Umayyads ruled the Arab world, including Jordan, from Damascus from A.D. 661 until A.D. 750 when they were replaced by the Abbasids of Baghdad.

UNITED ARAB KINGDOM (UAK). In 1972 King Hussein proposed the concept of a United Arab Kingdom made up of East Jordan (q.v.) and the Palestinian territories of the West Bank (q.v.) and perhaps Gaza (q.v.). The arrangement was to be federal, whereby considerable local authority would be accorded the Palestinians (q.v.) under the Hashemite (q.v.) monarchy. Israel controlled the West Bank and Gaza at the time (as it does as of this writing), and thus the plan came to naught. In the 1980s variations on this plan were raised once again, however the concept is usually described as a confederation between Jordan and Palestine (West Bank and Gaza).

UNITED NATIONS. *See* INTERNATIONAL ORGANIZA-
TIONS, UNITED NATIONS RELIEF AND WORKS
AGENCY FOR PALESTINE REFUGEES, UNITED
NATIONS RESOLUTION 242.

UNITED NATIONS RELIEF AND WORKS AGENCY FOR
PALESTINE REFUGEES (UNRWA). UNRWA is the U.N.
agency set up in the aftermath of the 1948–1949 Arab-Israeli war with a mandate to give assistance to the Palestinian refugees. It provides schooling and health and welfare
services for Palestinian refugees registered with UNRWA,
as well as housing for those who live in official refugee
camps administered by UNRWA. It operates in the Gaza
Strip, Jordan, Lebanon, Syria, and the West Bank. In Jordan, about 929,000 Palestinians were registered as official
refugees in 1990, or 30% of the Jordanian population.
About 223,000, or 6% of the Jordanian population, lived
in UNRWA refugee camps. *See also* PALESTINIANS,
REFUGEES.

UNITED NATIONS RESOLUTION 242.   U.N. Security
Council Resolution 242, passed on November 22, 1967,
established the basic principle for solving the Arab-Israeli
conflict (q.v.), whereby territory should be exchanged for
peace. More specifically, "withdrawal of Israeli armed
forces from territories occupied in the recent [1967] conflict" was balanced with "termination of all claims or states
of belligerency and respect for and acknowledgement of
the sovereignty, territorial integrity and political independence of every State in the area and their rights to live
in peace within secure and recognized boundaries free
from threats or acts of force." Diplomats have used this
resolution as the basis of many subsequent peace initiatives, including the Camp David Accords (q.v.), the Reagan
Middle East Peace Plan (q.v.), and the Bush/Baker initiative of 1989, and again in 1991.

UNITED STATES. The United States has maintained close relations with Jordan since the mid-1950s, especially as the British role was declining at that time. The U.S. policy toward Jordan has been largely governed by its interests in the Middle East: security vis-a-vis the Soviet Union, access to petroleum resources for the free world, and the security of Israel (q.v.). Jordan's traditionally moderate stance in the world and the Middle East and its frequent willingness to cooperate with the United States have also contributed to these positive relations. For years, though, King Hussein (q.v.) has sought a closer political and military relationship with the United States, but he has been continually frustrated by the terms of the United States relations with Israel. Nevertheless, his country maintains strong ties with America, especially in economic and educational terms.

Because the United States has been intricately involved in many major and minor Middle East developments, the United States appears throughout this dictionary. For significant references to the United States, *see also* INTRODUCTION: JORDAN'S HISTORY, ARAB-ISRAELI CONFLICT, CAMP DAVID ACCORDS, EISENHOWER DOCTRINE, JOHNSTON PLAN, PERSIAN GULF CRISIS AND WAR, REAGAN MIDDLE EAST PEACE PLAN, UNITED NATIONS RESOLUTION 242.

UNITED SYRIAN KINGDOM. The United Syrian Kingdom was the short-lived (March–July 1920) Arab government, based in Damascus and founded by Faisal ibn Hussein. Jordan was included in its borders. *See also* FAISAL IBN HUSSEIN, HASHEMITES.

UNIVERSITIES. *See* EDUCATION.

V

VILLAGERS. *See* FELLAH.

W

WADI AL-ARABA. The Wadi al-Araba is the deep, broad valley that stretches from the southern end of the Dead Sea halfway to the port of Aqaba.

WARS, ARAB-ISRAELI. On five occasions, the Arabs and Israel have gone to war: (1) In 1948–1949 Israel gained its independence, and Jordan acquired the West Bank. (2) Jordan did not join the 1956 war between Egypt and Israel. (3) In the 1967 war, also called the Six-Day War or the June War, Jordan, Egypt, and Syria, respectively, lost the West Bank, the Sinai, and the Golan Heights to Israeli military occupation. (4) In the 1973 war, also known as the October war, the Ramadan War, and the Yom Kippur War, Egypt regained a small portion of the Sinai and eventually all of it after it signed the 1979 peace treaty with Israel. Jordan participated minimally in the 1973 war, and then only on Syrian soil. (5) In 1982 Israel invaded Lebanon to fight the Palestine Liberation Organization. Jordan did not participate in this war. *See also* ARAB-ISRAELI CONFLICT, ISRAEL, PALESTINIANS.

WEST BANK. The West Bank, a part of historical Palestine (q.v.), lies to the west of the Jordan River and the Dead Sea. It came into political existence in 1948 when Jordanian troops occupied it during the first Arab-Israeli war. Today its population consists of about 1,000,000 Palestinians and 100,000 Jewish settlers. Some writers include Arab East Jerusalem in their definition of the West Bank, others do not. Many Israelis refer to the West Bank by its biblical designation, Judaea and Samaria.

After the West Bank was occupied by Jordanian forces during the 1948–1949 Arab-Israeli fighting, a series of political steps led to its inclusion in the Hashemite Kingdom of Jordan. Aside from general politicking and Jordanian administration, two key meetings of Palestinian notables were held—one in Amman and one in Jericho—during which the participants called for union of the East and West Banks. Despite the strong objections of a number of Arab countries, King Abdullah (q.v.) proceeded to act upon this request. He withdrew the military administration and replaced it with a civilian one. He also dissolved the parliament elected from only the East Bank (q.v.) and called for the election of a parliament whose members would be equally drawn from both banks. These elections were held in April 1950, and the parliament met later that month. On April 24, 1950, this body voted for the union of the West and East Banks under the kingship of Abdullah. The text of the resolution read:

First, [parliament's] support of complete unity between the two sides of the Jordan and their union into one state, which is the Hashemite Kingdom of Jordan, at whose head reigns King Abdullah Ibn al Husain, on a basis of constitutional representative government and equality of the rights and duties of all citizens.

Second, its reaffirmation of its intent to preserve the full Arab rights in Palestine, to defend those rights by all lawful means in the exercise of its natural rights but without prejudicing the final settlement of Palestine's just case within the sphere of national aspirations, inter-Arab cooperation and international justice.

By these actions, Jordan tripled its population and added about 2,100 square miles, or 5,440 square kilometers, to its territory. It also became integrally related to the Palestine problem and the Arab-Israeli conflict.

In the June 1967 Arab-Israeli war, Jordan lost the West Bank to Israeli military occupation. Despite this change of status, the government of Jordan maintained administrative and political ties to the West Bank, and the people maintained social and economic relations. In the summer of 1988, King Hussein announced that Jordan would disengage politically and administratively from the West Bank. This was in response to the political opinion expressed in the Palestinian *intifada* (q.v.), whereby the Palestinians of the West Bank and Gaza, inter alia, manifested their loyalty to the Palestine Liberation Organization (q.v.) and Palestinian nationalism and showed that they did not want Jordan to represent them. Despite the disengagement, Jordan has not renounced its claim to sovereignty over the West Bank. *See also* ALLON PLAN, ARAB-ISRAELI CONFLICT, CAMP DAVID ACCORDS, HUSSEIN IBN TALAL, ISRAEL, JERUSALEM, PALESTINIANS, UNITED NATIONS RESOLUTION 242.

WORLD WAR I. *See* INTRODUCTION: JORDAN'S HISTORY, ABDULLAH IBN HUSSEIN, GREAT BRITAIN, HASHEMITES.

Z

ZARQA. Zarqa is a large provincial capital northeast of Amman. The second largest city in Jordan, its economy is dominated by the military and industry.

BIBLIOGRAPHY

The purpose of this bibliography is to provide the reader with a substantive listing of the major works on Jordan. The emphasis is on works in English; however, key references in other languages, including Arabic, are listed as well. Because Jordan's history is intricately related to the Arab-Israeli conflict and the Palestinians and because the West Bank was at one time part of the country, a separate section on these closely related subjects is included in the bibliography.

The organization of the bibliography is as follows:

Bibliographies	89
Periodicals Relating to Jordan	91
Statistical References	92
General References: History, Politics, and Society	94
General References: Religion	103
Jordan: Archaeology	106
Jordan: History and Politics	106
Jordan and the Arab-Israeli Conflict, the Palestinians, and the West Bank	116
Jordan: Society and Development	132
Jordan: Economy	139

BIBLIOGRAPHIES

Abidi, Aqil. "Survey of Source Material: Select Arabic Source Material for the Modern Political History of Jordan." *International Studies* 4, no. 3 (January 1963): 317–28.

Atiyeh, George N. *The Contemporary Middle East, 1948–1973: A Selected and Annotated Bibliography.* Boston: G. K. Hall, 1975.

"Bibliography of Periodical Literature." *Middle East Journal* (1947–present). Published quarterly.

Cohen, E. "Recent Anthropological Studies of Middle Eastern Communities and Ethnic Groups." *Annual Review of Anthropology* 6 (1977): 315–47.

Geddes, Charles L., ed. *Books in English on Islam, Muhammad, and the Quran: A Selected, Annotated Bibliography.* Denver: American Institute of Islamic Studies, 1976.

The Middle East: The Strategic Hub. Washington: U.S. Department of the Army, 1979.

Mitchell, Richard P. *An Annotated Bibliography on the Modern History of the Near East.* Ann Arbor: University of Michigan Press, 1981.

———. *Politics and International Relations in the Middle East: An Annotated Bibliography.* Ann Arbor: University of Michigan Press, 1981.

Qazzaz, Ayad al-. *Women in the Middle East and North Africa: An Annotated Bibliography.* Middle East Monographs No. 2. Austin: University of Texas Press, 1977.

Shulz, Ann, ed. *International and Regional Politics in the Middle East and North Africa: A Guide to Informational Sources.* Detroit: Gale Research, 1977.

PERIODICALS RELATING TO JORDAN

American-Arab Affairs. Washington.

Al-Dustur. Amman. Daily.

Al-Fajr: Jerusalem, Palestinian Weekly. Jerusalem.

Foreign Broadcast Information Service: Middle East and North Africa (FBIS). Washington. Daily.

International Journal of Middle East Studies. New York.

Jerusalem Quarterly. Jerusalem.

Jordan Times. Amman. Daily.

Journal of Palestine Studies. Washington.

Journal of South Asian and Middle Eastern Studies. Villanova, Pa.

The Middle East. New York.

Middle East Economic Digest. London.

Middle East Economic Survey. Nicosia.

Middle East Insight. Cleveland.

Middle East International. London.

Middle East International. Washington.

Middle East Journal Washington.

Middle East Monitor. Ridgewood, N.J.

The Middle East Observer. Cairo.

Middle East Report (previously *MERIP Reports*). Washington.

Middle East Studies Association Bulletin. Tucson.

Middle Eastern Studies. London.

An-Nahar Arab Report and Memo. Beirut.

Near East Report. Washington.

New Outlook Middle East Monthly. Tel Aviv.

Al-Rai. Amman. Daily.

Sawt al-Sha'b. Amman. Daily.

Shu'un Filistiniya. Beirut.

Al-Urdun: A Jordan Newsletter. Washington.

STATISTICAL REFERENCES

Administered Territories Statistics Quarterly. Jerusalem: Central Bureau of Statistics, 1968–present.

Agricultural Census, 1980. Amman: Department of Statistics, 1980.

Annual Report. Amman: Central Bank of Jordan.

Annual Report. Amman: Department of Antiquities.

Annual Report. Amman: Department of Education.

Annual Report. Amman: Ministry of Industry and Trade.

Annual Report. Amman: Ministry of Labor.

Census of Agriculture, 1953. Amman: Department of Statistics, 1953.

Census of Population of the West Bank of the Jordan, Gaza Strip and Northern Sinai and Golan Heights. Jerusalem: Central Bureau of Statistics, 1967.

The Contribution of the West Bank in Jordan's Economy. Amman: Department of Statistics, 1969. (In Arabic)

Al-Dirasa al-Sina'iyya li'Am 1967 (Industrial Study for the Year 1965). Amman: Department of Statistics, 1967.

Employment Survey in Establishments Engaging 5 Persons or More, 1975. Amman: Department of Statistics, 1976. (In Arabic)

External Trade Statistics. Amman: Department of Statistics, various years.

First Census of Population and Housing. 4 vols. Amman: Department of Statistics, 1964.

'Ihsa'at al-Masakin li'Am 1952 (Housing Statistics for the Year 1952). Amman: Department of Statistics, 1952.

Industrial Survey, 1965. Amman: Department of Statistics, 1967. (In Arabic)

International Trade Statistics. Amman: General Department of Statistics, various years.

Monthly Statistical Bulletin. Amman: Central Bank of Jordan, Department of Research and Studies, various months and years.

The National Accounts, 1959–1967. Amman: Department of Statistics, n.d.

Palestinian Statistical Abstract. Damascus: Palestine Liberation Organization, Economic Department, Central Bureau of Statistics. Yearly.

Population and Internal Migration. Amman: Department of Statistics, 1967.

Population and Labour Force in the Agricultural Sector, 1967. Amman: Department of Statistics, 1968.

Quarterly Statistical Series. Amman: Central Bank of Jordan, various years.

Statistical Abstract of Israel. Jerusalem: Central Bureau of Statistics, 1968–present.

Statistical Bulletin for the West Bank and the Gaza Strip. Nablus: Rural Research Center, al-Najah National University, 1981–present.

Statistical Yearbook (Jordan). Amman: Department of Statistics, 1950–present.

Statistical Yearbook: Jordan Cooperative Organization. Amman: Jordan Cooperative Institute, various years.

Study of Labor Force, 1966. Amman: 1968. (In Arabic)

Al-Taqrir al-Sinawi 'an al-Ta'alim fi Madarisiha (Yearly Report on Education in Its Schools). Amman: Ministry of Education, yearly.

GENERAL REFERENCES: HISTORY, POLITICS, AND SOCIETY

Abdel-Malek, Anouar, ed. *Contemporary Arab Political Thought.* London: Zed Press, 1983.

Antonius, George. *The Arab Awakening: The Story of the Arab National Movement.* New York: G. P. Putnam's Sons, 1979.

Antoun, Richard T., and Iliya F. Harik. *Rural Politics and Social Change in the Middle East.* Bloomington: Indiana University Press, 1972.

Arjomand, Said Amir, ed. *From Nationalism to Revolutionary Islam: Essays on Social Movements in the Contemporary Near and Middle East.* Albany: State University of New York Press, 1984.

Aruri, Naseer H., ed. *The Middle East Crucible: Studies on the Arab-Israeli War of 1973.* Wilmette, Ill: Medina University Press International, 1975.

Badeau, John. *The American Approach to the Arab World.* New York: Harper and Row, 1967.

Beaumont, Peter, et al. *The Middle East: A Geographical Study.* New York: John Wiley, 1976.

Beck, Lois, and Nikki Keddie, eds. *Beyond the Veil: Women in the Middle East.* Cambridge: Harvard University Press, 1976.

_____ . *Women in the Muslim World.* Cambridge: Harvard University Press, 1978.

Bill, James A. *Politics in the Middle East.* 2nd ed. Boston: Little, Brown, 1984.

Bill, James A., and Carl Leiden. *The Middle East: Politics and Power.* 2nd ed. Boston: Little, Brown, 1979.

Boardman, Francis. *Institutions of Higher Learning in the Middle East.* Washington: Middle East Institute, 1977.

Brockelmann, Carl. *History of the Islamic Peoples*. London: Routledge and Kegan Paul, 1980.

Brown, L. Carl. *International Politics and the Middle East: Old Rules, Dangerous Game*. Princeton: Princeton University Press, 1984.

Brown, L. Carl, and Norman Itzkowitz. *Psychological Dimensions of Near Eastern Studies*. Princeton: Darwin Press, 1977.

Cantori, Louis, and Iliya Harik, eds. *Local Politics and Development in the Middle East*. Boulder, Colo.: Westview Press, 1984.

Chejne, Anwar G. *The Arabic Language: Its Role in History*. Minneapolis: University of Minnesota Press, 1969.

Chelkowski, Peter J., and Robert J. Pranger, eds. *Ideology and Power in the Middle East*. Durham, N.C.: Duke University Press, 1988.

Chomsky, Noam. *The Fateful Triangle: The United States, Israel and the Palestinians*. Boston: South End Press, 1983.

Costello, Vincent F. *Urbanization in the Middle East*. New York: Cambridge University Press, 1977.

Creswell, K. A. C. *Early Muslim Architecture*. New York: Hacker Art Books, 1979.

Dawisha, Karen, and Adeed Dawisha, eds. *The Soviet Union in the Middle East: Perspectives and Policies*. London: Holmes and Meier, 1982.

Economic Intelligence Unit. *EIU Annual Regional Review: The Middle East and North Africa*. London: Economic Intelligence Unit.

Eickelman, Dale. *The Middle East: An Anthropological Approach*. Englewood Cliffs, N.J.: Prentice-Hall, 1981.

Emery, James J., et al. *Technology Trade with the Middle East: Policy Issues and Economic Trends*. Boulder, Colo.: Westview Press, 1985.

Encyclopedia of Islam. Leiden: E. J. Brill, 1960–1978.

Faraah, T. E., ed. *Political Behavior in the Arab States*. Boulder, Colo.: Westview Press, 1983.

Fisher, Sydney N. *The Middle East: A History*. 3rd rev. ed. New York: Knopf, 1978.

Fisher, W. B. *The Middle East: A Physical, Social, and Regional Geography*. 7th ed. London: Methuen, 1978.

Freedman, Robert O., ed. *The Middle East Since Camp David*. Boulder, Colo.: Westview Press, 1984.

_____. *Soviet Policy Towards the Middle East Since 1970*. 3rd ed. New York: Praeger, 1982.

_____, ed. *World Politics and the Arab-Israeli Conflict*. New York: Pergamon Press, 1982.

Goldschmidt, Arthur. *A Concise History of the Middle East*. 3rd ed. Boulder, Colo.: Westview Press, 1988.

Haim, Sylvia G., ed. *Arab Nationalism: An Anthology*. Berkeley and Los Angeles: University of California Press, 1976.

Halpern, Manfred. *The Politics of Social Change in the Middle East and North Africa*. Princeton: Princeton University Press, 1963.

Hayes, John R., ed. *The Genius of Arab Civilization: Sources of Renaissance*. 2nd ed. Cambridge: MIT Press, 1983.

Hitti, Philip K. *History of the Arabs from the Earliest Times to the Present*. 10th ed. London: Macmillan, 1977.

_____ . *Islam and the West: A Historical and Cultural Survey*. Princeton: D. Van Nostrand, 1962.

Hourani, Albert. *The Emergence of the Modern Middle East*. Berkeley and Los Angeles: University of California Press, 1981.

Howard, Harry N. *The King-Crane Commission: An American Inquiry in the Middle East*. Beirut: Khayat, 1963.

Hudson, Michael C. *Arab Politics: The Search for Legitimacy*. New Haven: Yale University Press, 1977.

Hurewitz, Jacob C. *Diplomacy in the Near and Middle East,* vol. 1, *1535–1914;* vol. 2, *1914–1956*. Princeton: D. Van Nostrand, 1956.

_____ . *The Middle East and North Africa in World Politics: A Documentary Record*. New Haven: Yale University Press, 1975.

Ibrahim, Saad Eddin. *The New Arab Social Order*. Boulder, Colo.: Westview Press, 1982.

International Who's Who of the Arab World. London: International Who's Who of the Arab World, various years.

Issawi, Charles, ed. *The Economic History of the Middle East and North Africa*. New York: Columbia University Press, 1982.

Kahn, M. Wasiullah. *Education and Society in the Muslim World*. London: Hodder and Stoughton, 1981.

Karpat, Kemal H. *Political and Social Thought in the Contemporary Middle East*. Rev. ed. New York: Praeger, 1982.

Kerr, Malcolm. *The Arab Cold War: Gamal 'Abd al-Nasir and His Rivals, 1958–1970*. 3rd ed. New York: Oxford University Press, 1971.

Kerr, Malcolm, and Sayyid el-Yassin, eds. *Rich and Poor Nations in the Middle East*. Boulder, Colo.: Westview Press, 1982.

Khadduri, Majid. *Arab Contemporaries: The Role of Personalities in Politics*. Baltimore: Johns Hopkins University Press, 1973.

_____. *Arab Personalities in Politics*. Washington: Middle East Institute, 1981.

Klieman, A. S. *Foundations of British Policy in the Arab World: The Cairo Conference of 1921*. Baltimore: Johns Hopkins University Press, 1970.

Korany, Bahgat, and A. E. H. Dessouki, eds. *The Foreign Policies of Arab States*. Boulder, Colo.: Westview Press, 1984.

Lapidus, Ira M., ed. *The Middle Eastern Cities: A Symposium on Ancient, Islamic, and Contemporary Middle Eastern Urbanism*. Berkeley and Los Angeles: University of California Press, 1969.

Le Gassick, Trevor. *Major Themes in Modern Arabic Thought: An Anthology*. Ann Arbor: University of Michigan Press, 1979.

Legum, Colin, et al. *Middle East Contemporary Survey.* New York: Holmes and Meier Publishers, 1976–present.

Leitenberg, Milton, and Gabriel Sheffer, eds. *Great Power Intervention in the Middle East.* New York: Pergamon Press, 1979.

Lenczowski, George. *The Middle East in World Affairs.* 4th ed. Ithaca: Cornell University Press, 1982.

Levine, Victor, and Timothy Luke. *The Arab-African Connection.* Boulder, Colo.: Westview Press, 1979.

Levran, Aharon, and Zeev Eytan. *The Middle East Military Balance, 1986.* Boulder, Colo.: Westview Press, 1988.

Lewis, Bernard. *The Arabs in History.* 2nd ed. New York: Harper and Row, 1967.

Louis, William Roger. *British Empire in the Middle East, 1945–51: Arab Nationalism, the United States and Postwar Imperialism.* New York: Clarendon Press, 1984.

Mansfield, Peter. *The Arab World: A Comprehensive History.* New York: Thomas Y. Crowell, 1977.

_____ . *The Arabs.* Rev. ed. New York: Penguin Books, 1982.

McLaurin, Ronald D., ed. *The Political Role of Minority Groups in the Middle East.* New York: Praeger, 1979.

The Middle East and North Africa. London: Europa Publications. Annual.

Naff, Thomas, and F. W. Frey. "Water: An Emerging Issue in the Middle East?" *Annals of the American Academy of Political Science*, no. 482 (November 1985): 65–84.

Naff, Thomas, and Ruth C. Matson, eds. *Water in the Middle East: Cooperation or Conflict?* Boulder, Colo.: Westview Press, 1984.

Philby, H. St. John. *Arabian Days*. London: R. Hale, 1948.

_____. *Forty Years in the Wilderness*. London: R. Hale, 1957.

Pritchard, James B. *The Ancient Near East*. Princeton: Princeton University Press, 1973.

Ro'i, Yaacov. *The Limits to Soviet Power in the Middle East*. New York: St. Martin's Press, 1979.

Rugh, William A. *The Arab Press: News Media and Political Process in the Arab World*. Syracuse: Syracuse University Press, 1979.

Saadawi, Nawal el-. *The Hidden Face of Eve: Women in the Arab World*. Boston: Beacon Press, 1982.

Sachar, Howard M. *The Emergence of the Middle East, 1914–1924*. New York: Knopf, 1969.

Sharabi, Hisham. *Nationalism and Revolution in the Arab World*. Princeton: Van Nostrand, 1982.

Shiloh, Ailon. *Peoples and Cultures of the Middle East*. New York: Random House, 1969.

Simes, Dimitri. *Soviet Policy Toward the Middle East*. Washington: Johns Hopkins University School of Advanced International Studies, 1982.

Smith, Jane, ed. *Women in Contemporary Muslim Societies*. Lewisburg, Pa.: Bucknell University Press, 1980.

Starr, Joyce R., and Daniel C. Stoll, eds. *The Politics of Scarcity: Water in the Middle East*. Boulder, Colo.: Westview Press, 1988.

_____ . *U.S. Foreign Policy on Water Resources in the Middle East*. Washington: Center for Strategic and International Studies, 1987.

Stooky, Robert W. *America and the Arab States: An Uneasy Encounter*. New York: John Wiley, 1975.

Szyliowicz, Joseph S. *Education and Modernization in the Middle East*. Ithaca: Cornell University Press, 1973.

Tachau, Frank, ed. *Political Elites and Political Development in the Middle East*. Cambridge: Schenkman Publishers, 1975.

Tillman, Seth P. *The United States in the Middle East: Interests and Obstacles*. Bloomington: Indiana University Press, 1982.

Vatikiotis, P. J. *Arab and Regional Politics in the Middle East*. New York: St. Martin's Press, 1984.

Waddy, Charis. *Women in Muslim History*. New York: Longman, 1980.

Weinbaum, Marvin G. *Food, Development, and Politics in the Middle East*. Boulder, Colo.: Westview Press, 1982.

Zartman, I. William, ed. *Elites in the Middle East*. New York: Praeger, 1980.

GENERAL REFERENCES: RELIGION

Bewtts, Robert. *Christians in the Arab East: A Political Study*. Athens, Greece: Lycabettus Press, 1975.

Cragg, Kenneth. *The Call of the Minaret*. New York: Oxford University Press, 1964.

_____. *The House of Islam*. Belmont, Calif.: Dickenson Publishers, 1969.

_____. *Sandals at the Mosque: The Christian Presence amid Islam*. New York: Oxford University Press, 1969.

Cudsi, Alexander S., and Ali E. Dessouki, eds. *Islam and Power*. Baltimore: Johns Hopkins University Press, 1981.

Curtis, Michael, ed. *Religion and Politics in the Middle East*. Boulder, Colo.: Westview Press, 1981.

Dawisha, Adeed, ed. *Islam in Foreign Policy*. New York: Cambridge University Press, 1983.

Dawood, N. J., trans. *The Koran*. Rev. 4th ed. New York: Penguin Books, 1974.

Dekmejian, R. Hrair. *Islam in Revolution: Fundamentalism in the Arab World*. Syracuse, N.Y.: Syracuse University Press, 1985.

Dessouki, Ali E. H., ed. *Islamic Resurgence in the Arab World*. New York: Praeger, 1982.

Donohue, John J., and John Esposito, eds. *Islam in Transition: Muslim Perspectives*. New York: Oxford University Press, 1982.

Esposito, John L., ed. *Islam and Development: Religion and Sociopolitical Change*. Syracuse, N.Y.: Syracuse University Press, 1980.

_____. *Islam and Politics*. Syracuse, N.Y.: Syracuse University Press, 1984.

_____, ed. *Voices of Resurgent Islam*. New York: Oxford University Press, 1983.

_____. *Women in Muslim Family Law*. Syracuse, N.Y.: Syracuse University Press, 1982.

Gibb, Sir H. A. R. *Mohammedanism: An Historical Survey*. 2nd ed. New York: Oxford University Press, 1962.

Goiten, S. D. *Jews and Arabs: Their Contact Through the Ages*. 3rd rev. ed. New York: Schocken Books, 1974.

Guillaume, Alfred. *Islam*. Harmondsworth: Penguin Books, 1982.

Haddad, Yvonne Y. *Contemporary Islam and the Challenge of History*. Albany: State University of New York Press, 1982.

Hibri, Azizah al-, ed. *Women and Islam*. New York: Pergamon Press, 1982.

Hodgson, Marshall G. S. *The Venture of Islam: Conscience and History in a World Civilization*. Chicago: University of Chicago Press, 1975.

Holt, P. M., et al., eds. *The Cambridge History of Islam*. Cambridge: Cambridge University Press, 1970.

Hourani, Albert, ed. *Essays on Islamic Philosophy and Science.* Albany: State University of New York Press, 1975.

Hussain, Freda, ed. *Muslim Women: The Ideal and Contextual Realities.* New York: St. Martin's Press, 1984.

Khadduri, Majid. *The Islamic Concept of Justice.* Baltimore: Johns Hopkins University Press, 1984.

Khadduri, Majid, and Herbert J. Liebesny, eds. *Origin and Development of Islamic Law.* New York: AMS Press, 1984.

Lewis, Bernard. *Islam from the Prophet Muhammad to the Capture of Constantinople.* Vol. 1, *Politics and War;* vol. 2, *Religion and Society.* New York: Harper and Row, 1975.

_____. *Race and Color in Islam.* New York: Harper and Row, 1975.

Lings, Martin. *Muhammad: His Life Based on the Earliest Sources.* London: Allen and Unwin, 1983.

Mortimer, Edward. *Faith and Power: The Politics of Islam.* New York: Vintage Books, 1982.

Piscatori, James, ed. *Islam in the Political Process.* London: Cambridge University Press, 1983.

Savory, R. M., ed. *Introduction to Islamic Civilization.* New York: Cambridge University Press, 1976.

Sivan, Emmanuel. *Radical Islam, Medieval Theology and Modern Politcs.* New Haven: Yale University Press, 1985.

Stoddard, Philip H., et al. *Change and the Muslim World.* Syracuse, N.Y.: Syracuse University Press, 1981.

Voll, John O., ed. *Islam: Continuity and Change in the Modern World*. Boulder, Colo.: Westview Press, 1982.

Watt, William Montgomery. *The Formative Period of Islamic Thought*. Edinburgh: Edinburgh University Press, 1973.

JORDAN: ARCHAEOLOGY

Albright, William F. *Archaeology of Palestine*. Gloucester, Mass.: Peter Smith, 1972.

Glueck, Nelson. *Deities and Dolphins: The Story of the Nabataeans*. New York: Farrar, Straus and Giroux, 1965.

Harding, G. Lankester. *The Antiquities of Jordan*. New York: Thomas Y. Crowell, 1959.

_____ . *The Antiquities of Jordan*. Rev. ed. New York: Praeger, 1967.

Hoade, Eugene. *East of the Jordan*. Jerusalem: Franciscan Printing Press, 1966.

Hollis, Christopher, and Ronald Brownrigg. *Holy Places: Jewish, Christian, and Muslim Monuments in the Holy Land*. London: Weidenfeld and Nicolson, 1969.

Khouri, Rami G. *The Antiquities of the Jordan Rift Valley*. Amman: Al-Kutba Publishers, 1988.

Wolf, Betty Hartman. *Journey Through the Holy Land*. Garden City, N.Y.: Doubleday, 1968.

JORDAN: HISTORY AND POLITICS

Abdullah, H.M. King. *Memoirs of King Abdullah of Transjordan*. London: Oxford University Press, 1950.

_____. *My Memoirs Completed*. Washington: ACLS, 1954.

Abidi, Aqil. *Jordan: A Political Study, 1948–57*. London: Asia Publishing House, 1965.

Abu Jaber, Kamel S. *The Arab Ba'ath Socialist Party: History, Ideology and Organization*. Rochester, N.Y.: Syracuse University Press, 1966.

_____. "The Legislature of the Hashemite Kingdom of Jordan: A Study in Political Development." *Muslim World* 59, no. 1(1969): 220–50.

Aruri, Naseer H. *Jordan: A Study in Political Development, 1921–1965*. The Hague: Martinus Nijhoff, 1972.

Bulus, Salman. *Five Years in East Jordan*. Jerusalem, 1929. (In Arabic).

Burckhardt, J. L. *Travels in Syria and the Holy Land*. London: Murray, 1822.

Burns, General E. L. M. *Between Arab and Israeli*. London: Harrap, 1962.

Canaan, Taufiq. "The Saqr Bedouin." *Journal of Palestine Oriental Society* 16 (1936): 21–32.

Carr, Winifred. *Hussein's Kingdom of Jordan*. London: Leslie Frewin, 1966.

Cordesman, Anthony H. *Jordanian Arms and the Middle East Balance*. Washington: Middle East Institute, 1983.

Dann, Uriel. "Regime and Opposition in Jordan Since 1949." In Menachem Milson, ed. *Society and Structure: Political Structure in the Arab World*. Van Leer Foundation Series. New York: Humanities Press, 1973.

_____. *Studies in the History of Transjordan, 1920–1949: The Making of a State*. Boulder, Colo.: Westview Press, 1984.

Day, Arthur. *East Bank/West Bank: Jordan and the Prospects for Peace*. New York: Council on Foreign Relations, 1986.

Deardon, Anne. *Jordan*. London: Robert Hale, 1958.

Dissard, J. "Les migrations et les vicissitudes de la tribu des 'Amer." *Revue Biblique*, January 18, 1905, 410–25.

Doughty, C. M. *Travels in Arabia Deserta*. Cambridge: Cambridge University Press, 1888.

Edroos, Brigadier Syed Ali el-. *The Hashemite Arab Army, 1908–1979: An Appreciation and Analysis of Military Operations*. Amman: The Publishing Committee, 1980.

Faddah, Mohammad Ibrahim. *The Middle East in Transition: A Study of Jordan's Foreign Policy*. New York: Asia Publishing House, 1974.

Farra, Muhammad el-. *Years of No Decision*. London: KPI, 1987.

Forder, A. *In Brigands' Hands and Turkish Prisons, 1914–18*. London: Marshall, 1919.

_____. *Ventures Among the Arab in Desert, Tent, and Town*. Boston: Hartshorn, 1905.

_____. *With the Arabs in Tent and Town*. London: Marshall, 1902.

Forrest, Alfred C. *The Unholy Land*. Toronto: McClelland and Stewart, 1971.

Forsythe, David P. *United Nations Peacekeeping: The Concili-ation Commission for Palestine*. Baltimore: Johns Hopkins University Press, 1972.

Furlonge, Geoffrey. "Jordan Today." *Royal Central Asian Journal* 53 (October 1966): 277–85.

Gabriel, Richard A., and Alan S. MacDougall. "Jordan." In Richard A. Gabriel, ed. *Fighting Armies: Antagonists in the Middle East—A Combat Assessment*. London: Greenwood Press, 1983.

Garfinkle, Adam M. "Negotiating by Proxy: Jordanian Foreign Policy and U.S. Options in the Middle East." *Orbis* 24 (Winter 1981): 847–80.

Glubb, Sir John Bagot. *Britain and the Arabs: A Study of Fifty Years*. London: Hodder, 1959.

_____. *The Changing Scenes of Life: An Autobiography*. London: John Murray, 1983.

_____. *A Soldier with the Arabs*. New York: Harper and Row, 1967.

_____. *The Story of the Arab Legion*. London: Hodder, 1948.

_____. *Syria, Lebanon, Jordan*. New York: Walker, 1967.

Goichon, A. M. *Jordanie Réelle*. 2 vols. Paris: De Brouwer, 1967, 1972.

Gubser, Peter. "Jordan: Balancing Pluralism and Authoritari-anism." In P. Chelkowski and R. Pranger, eds. *Ideology and Power in the Middle East*. Durham, N.C.: Duke University Press, 1988.

_____ . *Jordan: Crossroads of Middle Eastern Events*. Boulder, Colo.: Westview Press, 1983.

_____ . *Politics and Change in Al-Karak, Jordan: A Study of a Small Arab Town and Its District*. London: Oxford University Press, 1973.

_____ . *Politics and Change in Al-Karak, Jordan*. Boulder, Colo.: Westview Press Encore Editions, 1985.

Gubser, Peter, with M. Peck. "Jordan and Saudi Arabia: Monarchies at the Crossroads?" *Worldview*, January 1984.

Hassan, H. R. H. Prince. *Search for Peace*. New York: St. Martin's Press, 1984.

Hijazi, Nayif, and Mahmud Atallah. *Jordanian Personalities*. Amman, 1973. (In Arabic)

Hill, G. *With the Beduins*. London: Fisher Unwin, 1891.

Hussein, H.R.M. King. *My Profession as a King*. Amman: Ghaleb Toukan, 1978. (In Arabic)

_____ . *My War with Israel*. As told to, and with additional material by, Vick Vance and Pierre Lauer. New York: William Morrow, 1969.

_____ . *The Palestine Question*. Amman: Ministry of Information, 1965.

_____ . "Reflections on an Epilogue: *Al-Takmilah* to the Memoirs of King Abdullah Ibn Al-Hussein." *Middle East Journal* 32, no. 1 (Winter 1978): 79–86.

_____ . *Twenty-five Years of History: The Complete Collection of H.M. King Hussein Ben Talal's Speeches, 1952–1977.* London: Samir Mutawi, 1979. (In Arabic)

_____ . *Uneasy Lies the Head: The Autobiography of His Majesty King Hussein I of the Hashemite Kingdom of Jordan.* New York: Bernard Geis Associates, 1962.

Irby, C. *Travels in Egypt and Nubia and Asia Minor During the Years 1817 and 1818.* London: T. White, 1823.

Jarvis, Claude Scudamore. *Arab Command: The Biography of F. G. Peake Pasha.* London: Hutchinson, 1943.

Johnston, Sir Charles. *The Brink of Jordan.* London: Hamilton, 1972.

Jureidini, Paul A., and R. D. McLaurin. *Jordan: The Impact of Social Change on the Role of Tribes.* New York: Praeger, 1984.

Kaplan, Stephen S. "United States Aid and Regime Maintenance in Jordan, 1957–1973." *Public Policy* 23, no. 2 (Spring 1975): 189–217.

Kazziha, Walid. *The Social History of Southern Syria (Trans-Jordan) in the Nineteenth and Early Twentieth Century.* Beirut, 1972.

Kirkbride, Sir A. *A Crackle of Thorns.* London: Murray, 1956.

_____ . *From the Wings: Amman Memoirs, 1947–1951.* London: Frank Cass, 1976.

Kurd, A. A. el-, *The Hashemites.* Amman, 1967.

Laqueur, Walter Z. "Communism in Jordan." *World Today* 12, no. 3 (March 1956): 109–19.

Lawrence, T. E. *Seven Pillars of Wisdom*. Garden City, N.Y.: Doubleday, 1935.

Lias, Godfrey. *Glubb's Legion*. London: Evans Brothers, 1956.

Luke, Harry, and Edward Keith-Roach. *The Handbook of Palestine and Trans-Jordan*. London: Macmillan, 1930.

Lunt, James D. *Glubb Pasha—A Biography: Lieutenant-General Sir John Bagot Glubb, Commander of the Arab Legion, 1939–1956*. London: Harvill Press, 1984.

_____. *Hussein of Jordan*. New York: William Morrow, 1989.

Mady, Munib al-, and Sulayman Musa. *Ta'rikh al-'Urdun fi al-Qarn al-'Ishrin* (History of Jordan in the Twentieth Century). [Amman], 1959.

Médebielle, P. *Kérak: Histoire de la mission*. Jerusalem: Imp. du Patriarcat Latin, 1961.

Merrill, S. *East of the Jordan*. London: Bentley, 1881.

Monroe, Elizabeth. *Philby of Arabia*. London: Faber and Faber, 1973.

Morris, James. *The Hashemite Kings*. New York: Pantheon, 1959.

Musa, Sulayman. *The Establishment of the Jordanian Emirate*. Amman, 1972. (In Arabic)

_____. "A Matter of Principle: King Hussein of the Hijaz and the Arabs of Palestine." *International Journal of Middle East Studies* 9, no. 2 (May 1978): 183–94.

_____. *T. E. Lawrence: An Arab View*. London: Oxford University Press, 1966.

Nassar, Fuad. "Jordan's Road to Complete Liberation, Democracy and Social Progress." *World Marxist Review* 9, no. 1 (January 1966): 48–52.

Nevo, Joseph. "Is There a Jordanian Entity?" *Jerusalem Quarterly*, no. 16 (Summer 1980): 98–110.

Nutting, Anthony. *Lawrence of Arabia: The Man and the Motive*. New York: Clarkson N. Potter, 1961.

Nyrop, Richard F., et al. *Jordan: A Country Study*. Washington: Foreign Area Studies Division, American University, 1980.

Patai, R. *The Kingdom of Jordan*. Princeton: Princeton University Press, 1958.

Peake, Frederick. *History and Tribes of Jordan*. Miami, Fla.: Miami University Press, 1958.

_____. *The History of East Jordan*. Jerusalem, 1935.

_____. "Transjordan." *Journal of the Royal Central Asian Society* 26 (July 1939): 375–96.

Perowne, Stewart. "The Arab Legion." *Geographical Magazine* 27 (1954): 352–58.

Philby, H. St. John. "Trans-Jordan." *Journal of the Royal Central Asian Society* 11 (June 1924).

Rustow, Dankwart A. *Hussein: A Biography*. London: Barrie and Jenkins, 1972.

Salah, Peter, and Mohammad Huneidi. "The Jordanian Perception of the Conflict." *Middle East Review*, nos. 5 and 6 (Fall 1975): 45–53.

Sanger, Richard H. *Where the Jordan Flows*. Washington: Middle East Institute, 1963.

Satloff, Robert B. *The Troubles on the East Bank: Challenges to the Domestic Stability of Jordan*. New York: Praeger, 1986.

Saulcy, F. de. *Voyage autour de la Mer Morte*, vol. 1. Paris: Gide et Baudry, 1853.

Sayigh, Anis. *The Hashemite and the Palestine Question*. Beirut, 1966.

Seton, C. R. W., ed. *Legislation of Transjordan, 1918–1930*. London: Crown Agents, [1931].

Shlaim, Avi. *Collusion Across the Jordan: King Abdullah, the Zionist Movement and the Partition of Palestine*. London: Oxford University Press, 1988.

Shwadran, Benjamin. *Jordan: A State of Tension*. New York: Council for Middle Eastern Affairs Press, 1959.

Simon, Reeva S. "The Hashemite 'Conspiracy': Hashemite Unity Attempts, 1921–1958." *International Journal of Middle East Studies* 5, no. 3 (June 1974): 314–27.

Sinai, Anne, and Allen Pollack, eds. *The Hashemite Kingdom of Jordan and the West Bank: A Handbook*. New York: American Academic Association for Peace in the Middle East, 1977.

Snow, Peter. *Hussein: A Biography*. Washington: Robert B. Luce, 1972.

Sparrow, Gerald. *Hussein of Jordan*. London: George C. Harrap, 1960.

_____ . *Modern Jordan*. London: Allen and Unwin, 1961.

Stevens, Georgiana. *Jordan River Partition*. Stanford: Hoover Institute, 1965.

Tokun, Baha Uddin. *A Short History of Transjordan*. London: Luzac, 1945.

_____ . "Transjordan: Past, Present, and Future." *Journal of the Royal Central Asian Society* 31 (July-October 1944): 253–64.

Tristram, H. B. *The Land of Moab*. London: Murray, 1873.

Vatikiotis, P. J. *Politics and the Military in Jordan: A Study of the Arab Legion, 1921–1957*. New York: Praeger, 1967.

Viorst, Milton. "Jordan: A Moderate Role." *Atlantic Monthly*, March 1981.

Wilson, Mary C. *King Abdullah, Britain and the Making of Jordan*. Cambridge: Cambridge University Press, 1987.

Wolf, Betty Hartman. *Journey Through the Holy Land*. Garden City, N.Y.: Doubleday, 1968.

Wright, Esmond. "Abdullah's Jordan: 1947–1951." *Middle East Journal* 5, no. 4 (Autumn 1951): 439–60.

Yorke, Valerie. *Domestic Politics and Regional Security: Jordan, Syria and Israel*. London: Gower, for the International Institute for Strategic Studies, 1988.

York, Peter. *The Arab Legion*. London: Osprey Publishing, 1972.

_____. *Bedouin Command with the Arab Legion, 1953–56*. London: W. Kimber, 1956.

Zirikli, Khayr al-Din al-. *Two Years in Amman*. Cairo, 1925. (In Arabic)

JORDAN AND THE ARAB-ISRAELI CONFLICT, THE PALESTINIANS, AND THE WEST BANK

Abboushi, Wasif. *The Unmaking of Palestine*. Outwell, England: Menas Press, 1985.

Abd al-Hadi, Mahdi. *The Palestinian Question and Proposals for Political Solutions, 1934–1974*. Beirut: Al-Maktabah al-Asriyah, 1975. (In Arabic)

Abu Hijleh, A. *The Industrial Sector in the Occupied Territories and the Effects of Israeli Occupation*. Amman: Central Bank of Jordan, 1981. (In Arabic)

_____. *Studies in the Economies of the Occupied Territories*. Amman: Central Bank of Jordan, 1981. (In Arabic)

Abu-Lughod, Ibrahim, ed. *The Transformation of Palestine: Essays on the Origin and Development of the Arab-Israeli Conflict*. Evanston, Ill.: Northwestern University Press, 1971.

Adams, Michael. "Israel's Treatment of the Arabs in the Occupied Territories." *Journal of Palestine Studies* 6 (Winter 1977): 19–40.

Allon, Yigal. "Israel: The Case for Defensible Borders." *Foreign Affairs* 55 (October 1976): 38–53.

American Friends Service Committee. *A Compassionate Peace: A Future for the Middle East*. New York: Hill and Wang, 1982.

Arabs Under Israeli Occupation, 1981. Washington: Institute for Palestine Studies, 1984.

Aronson, Geoffrey. *Creating Facts: Israel, Palestinians and the West Bank*. Washington: Institute for Palestine Studies, 1987.

Aruri, Naseer. *Occupation: Israel over Palestine*. Belmont, Mass.: AAUG Press, 1983.

Awartani, Hisham. *Agriculture in the West Bank: A New Outlook*. Nablus: Al-Najah National University, 1978.

_____ . *A Survey of Industries in the West Bank and Gaza*. Birzeit: Birzeit University Publications, 1979.

Azar, Edward E., and R. D. McLaurin. *The Demographic Imperative in Arab-Israeli Settlement*. Alexandria, Va.: Abbott Associates, 1977.

Bahiri, Simcha. *Industrialization in the West Bank and Gaza*. Boulder, Colo.: Westview Press, 1988.

Bailey, Clinton. "Changing Attitudes Toward Jordan in the West Bank." *Middle East Journal* 32 (Spring 1978): 155–66.

_____ . *Jordan's Palestinian Challenge, 1948–1983: A Political History*. Boulder, Colo.: Westview Press, 1984.

Ben-Dor, Gabriel, ed. *The Palestinians and the Middle East Conflict*. Ramat-Gan, Israel: Turtledove Publishing, 1978.

Ben Shahar, Haim, et al. *Economic Structure and Development Prospects of the West Bank and Gaza Strip.* Santa Monica: Rand Corporation, 1971.

Benvenisti, Meron. *1986 Report: Demographic, Economic, Legal, Social, and Political Developments in the West Bank.* Jerusalem: Jerusalem Post, 1986.

_____. *The West Bank Data Project: A Survey of Israel's Policies.* Washington: American Enterprise Institute, 1984.

Benvenisti, Meron, and Shlomo Khayat. *The West Bank and Gaza Atlas.* Jerusalem: West Bank Data Base Project and Jerusalem Post, 1988.

Benvenisti, Meron, et al. *The West Bank Handbook: A Political Lexicon.* Boulder, Colo.: Westview Press, 1986.

Bergman, Arie. *Economic Growth in the Administered Areas, 1968–1973.* Jerusalem: Bank of Israel, Research Department, 1975.

_____. *The Economy of the Administered Areas, 1974–1975.* Jerusalem: Bank of Israel, 1976.

Bovis, H. Eugene. *The Jerusalem Question, 1917–1968.* Stanford: Hoover Institution Press, 1971.

British Consulate. *West Bank: Water Resources and Their Exploitation.* Jerusalem, 1978.

Brookings Institution. *Toward Peace in the Middle East: Report of a Study Group.* Washington: Brookings Institution, 1975.

Brown, L. Dean. *The Land of Palestine: West Bank, Not East Bank*. Washington: Middle East Institute, 1984.

Buehring, Edward H. *The U.N. and the Palestinian Refugee: A Study in Non-Territorial Administration*. Bloomington: Indiana University Press, 1971.

Bull, Vivian. *The West Bank: Is It Viable?* Lexington, Mass.: Lexington Books, 1975.

Carter, Jimmy. *The Blood of Abraham: Insights into the Middle East*. Boston: Houghton Mifflin, 1985.

Cattan, Henry. *Palestine and International Law: The Legal Aspects of the Arab-Israeli Conflict*. London: Longman, 1973.

Cobban, Helena. *The Palestine Liberation Organization: People, Power and Politics*. New York: Cambridge University Press, 1984.

Cohen, Amnon. "The Changing Patterns of West Bank Politics." *Jerusalem Quarterly*, no. 5 (Fall 1977): 105–13.

_____. "Does a 'Jordan Option' Still Exist?" *Jerusalem Quarterly*, no. 16 (Summer 1980): 111–20.

_____. "The Jordanian Communist Party in the West Bank, 1950–60." In M. Confino and S. Shamir, eds., *The USSR and the Middle East*. New Brunswick, N.J.: Transaction Publishers, 1973.

_____. *Political Parties in the West Bank Under the Jordanian Regime, 1949–1967*. Ithaca: Cornell University Press, 1982.

Cohen, Saul. *The Geopolitics of Israel's Border Question*. Boulder, Colo.: Westview Press, 1988.

Cooley, John K. *Green March, Black September: The Story of the Palestinian Arabs*. London: Frank Cass, 1978.

Curtis, Michael, et al. *The Palestinians: People, History, Politics*. New Brunswick, N.J.: Transaction Publishers, 1975.

Davies, Philip E. "The Educated West Bank Palestinians." *Journal of Palestine Studies* 8 (Spring 1979): 65–80.

Davis, John H. *The Evasive Peace: A Study of the Zionist-Arab Problem*. Cleveland: Dillon/Liederbach, 1976.

Davis, Uri, et al. "Israel's Water Policies." *Journal of Palestine Studies* 9 (Winter 1980): 3–31.

Day, Arthur. *East Bank/West Bank: Jordan and the Prospects for Peace*. New York: Council on Foreign Relations, 1986.

Dodd, Peter, and Halim Barakat. *River Without Bridges: A Study of the Exodus of the 1967 Palestinian Arab Refugees*. Beirut: Institute for Palestine Studies, 1969.

Dupuy, Trevor. *Elusive Victory: The Arab-Israeli Wars, 1947–1974*. New York: Harper and Row, 1979.

Elazar, Daniel J., ed. *Governing Peoples and Territories*. Philadelphia: Institute for the Study of Human Issues, 1982.

———. *Judea, Samaria, and Gaza: Views on the Present and Future*. Washington: American Enterprise Institute, 1982.

———. *Self Rule/Shared Rule: Federal Solutions to the Middle East Conflict*. Ramat Gan, Israel: Turtledove Publishing, 1979.

Forsythe, David P. "UNRWA, the Palestinian Refugees, and World Politics." *International Organization* 25, no. 1, 1972, pp. 26–45.

Gabbay, Rony E. *A Political Study of the Arab-Jewish Conflict: The Arab Refugee Problem—A Case Study.* Geneva: E. Droz, 1959.

Gazit, Shlomo. "Early Attempts at Establishing West Bank Autonomy: The 1968 Case Study." *Harvard Journal of Law and Public Policy* 3 (1980): 129–53.

Gerson, Allan. *Israel, the West Bank and International Law.* London: Frank Cass, 1978.

Gharaibeh, Fawzi A. *The Economies of the West Bank and Gaza Strip.* Boulder, Colo.: Westview Press, 1985.

Gilmour, David. *Dispossessed: The Ordeal of the Palestinians.* London: Sphere Books, 1982.

Graham-Brown, Sarah. *Education, Repression, Liberation: Palestinians.* London: World University Service, 1984.

Grossman, David. *The Yellow Wind.* New York: Farrar, Straus and Giroux, 1988.

Gubser, Peter. "Palestinian Continuity" (essay review article). *Journal of Palestine Studies*, Autumn 1978.

_____ . *West Bank and Gaza Economic and Social Development: Now and the Future.* Middle East Problem Paper No. 20. Washington: Middle East Institute, 1979.

Hadawi, Sami. *Bitter Harvest: Palestine Between 1914 and 1967.* New York: New World Press, 1967.

Halabi, Rafik. *The West Bank Story*, trans. Ina Friedman. New York: Harcourt Brace Jovanovich, 1982.

Harris, William W. *Taking Root: Israeli Settlement in the West Bank, the Golan, and Gaza-Sinai, 1967–1980.* New York: Research Studies Press, 1980.

Hassan ibn Talal, H.R.H., Crown Prince of Jordan. *Palestinian Self-Determination: A Study of the West Bank and Gaza Strip.* New York: Quartet Books, 1981.

Heller, Mark. *A Palestinian State: The Implications for Israel.* Cambridge: Harvard University Press, 1983.

Herzog, Chaim. *The Arab-Israel Wars.* New York: Random House, 1982.

Hilal, Jamil. *The West Bank: Social and Economic Structure, 1948–1974.* Beirut: Palestine Liberation Organization Research Center, 1975. (In Arabic)

Hudson, Michael C., ed. *Alternative Approaches to the Arab-Israeli Conflict: A Comparative Analysis of the Principal Actors.* Washington: CCAS, Georgetown University, 1984.

Hurewitz, J. C. *The Struggle for Palestine.* New York: W. W. Norton, 1950.

Hussein, H.R.M. King. *My War with Israel.* As told to, and with additional material by, Vick Vance and Pierre Lauer. New York: William Morrow, 1969.

_____. *The Palestine Question.* Amman: Ministry of Information, 1965.

Hutchinson, Elmo H. *Violent Truce: A Military Observer Looks at the Arab-Israeli Conflict, 1951–1955*. London: John Calder, 1955.

Ingram, Doreen. *Palestine Papers, 1917–1922: Seeds of Conflict*. London: Cox and Wyman, 1972.

International Documents of Palestine. Washington: Institute for Palestine Studies. Annual.

Ionides, M. G. "The Disputed Waters of the Jordan." *Middle East Journal*, no. 2 (Spring 1953): 153–64.

Jaffal, Mustafa. *The Palestinian Working Class and the Labor Union Movements in the West Bank and the Gaza Strip*. Beirut: Dar al-Jamahir, 1980.

Kerr, Malcolm H., ed. *The Elusive Peace in the Middle East*. Albany: State University of New York, 1976.

Khalidi, Walid, ed. *From Haven to Conquest: Readings in Zionism and the Palestine Problem Until 1948*. Washington: Institute for Palestine Studies, 1987.

———. "Thinking the Unthinkable: A Sovereign Palestinian State." Foreign Affairs 56, no. 4 (October 1973): 695–713.

Khouri, Fred J. *The Arab-Israeli Dilemma*. 3rd ed. Syracuse, N.Y.: Syracuse University Press, 1985.

Klieman, Aaron S. "Israel, Jordan, Palestine: The Search for a Durable Peace." *Washington Papers* 9, no. 83 (1981).

Kuroda, Alice, and Yasumasa Kuroda. *Palestinians Without Palestine: A Study of Political Socialization Among Palestinian Youths*. Washington: University Press of America, 1978.

Kuttab, Johnathan, and Raja Shehadeh. *Civilian Administration in the Occupied West Bank: Analysis of Israeli Military Government Order No. 947*. Ramallah, West Bank (Israel): Law in the Service of Man, 1982.

Laqueur, Walter Z. *The Road to War, 1967*. London: Secker and Warburg, 1968.

Lerner, Abba, and Haim Ben-Shahar. *The Economics of Efficiency and Growth: Lessons from Israel and the West Bank*. Cambridge, Mass.: Ballinger, 1975.

Lesch, Ann M. *Arab Politics in Palestine, 1917–1939: The Frustration of a Nationalist Movement*. Ithaca: Cornell University Press, 1979.

_____ . "Israeli Deportation of Palestinians from the West Bank and the Gaza Strip, 1967–1978." *Journal of Palestine Studies* 8 (Winter 1979): 101–31; (Spring 1979): 81–112.

_____ . "Israeli Settlements in the Occupied Territories." *Journal of Palestine Studies* 7 (Autumn 1977): 26–47; 8 (Autumn 1978): 100–119.

_____ . *Israel's Occupation of the West Bank: The First Two Years*. Santa Monica: Rand Corporation, 1970.

_____ . *Political Perceptions of the Palestinians on the West Bank and the Gaza Strip*. Washington: Middle East Institute, 1980.

Litani, Yehuda. "Leadership in the West Bank and Gaza." *Jerusalem Quarterly*, no. 14 (Winter 1980): 99–109.

Lukacs, Yehuda, ed. *Documents on the Israeli-Palestinian Conflict, 1967–1983*. New York: Cambridge University Press, 1984.

Mallison, Sally V., and W. Thomas Mallison. *Settlements and the Law: A Juridical Analysis of the Israeli Settlements in the Occupied Territories.* Washington: American Educational Trust, 1982.

Maoz, Moshe. *Palestinian Leadership on the West Bank: The Changing Role of the Arab Mayors Under Jordan and Israel.* London: Frank Cass, 1984.

_____ , ed. *Palestinian Arab Politics.* Jerusalem: Jerusalem Academic Press, 1975.

Meron, Raphael. *The Economy of the Administered Areas, 1977–1978.* Jerusalem: Bank of Israel, Research Department, 1980.

Migdal, Joel S., ed. *Palestinian Society and Politics.* Princeton: Princeton University Press, 1980.

Miller, Aaron D. "Jordan and the Arab-Israeli Conflict: The Hashemite Predicament." *Orbis,* Winter 1986.

_____ . *The PLO and the Politics of Survival.* New York: Praeger, 1983.

Mishal, Shaul. *West Bank/East Bank: The Palestinians in Jordan, 1949–1967.* New Haven: Yale University Press, 1978.

Monroe, Elizabeth. "The West Bank: Palestinian or Israeli?" *Middle East Journal* 31 (Autumn 1977): 397–412.

Moore, John N., ed. *The Arab-Israeli Conflict.* 3 vols. Princeton: Princeton University Press, 1973.

_____ , ed. *The Arab-Israeli Conflict: Readings and Documents.* Princeton: Princeton University Press, 1977.

Morris, Benny. *The Birth of the Palestinian Refugee Problem, 1947–49*. London: Cambridge University Press, 1988.

Mutawi, Samir A. *Jordan in the 1967 War*. Cambridge: Cambridge University Press, 1987.

Nakhleh, Emile. *The West Bank and Gaza: Toward the Making of a Palestinian State*. Washington: American Enterprise Institute, 1979.

————, ed. *A Palestinian Agenda for the West Bank and Gaza*. Washington: American Enterprise Institute, 1980.

Nakhleh, Khalil, and Clifford Wright. *After the Palestine-Israel War: Limits to U.S. and Israeli Policy*. Belmont, Mass.: Institute for Arab Studies, 1983.

Nakhleh, Khalil, and Elia Zureik, eds. *The Sociology of the Palestinians*. New York: St. Martin's Press, 1980.

Nazzal, Nafez. *The Palestinian Exodus from Galilee, 1948*. Beirut: Institute for Palestine Studies, 1978.

Neff, Donald. *Warriors for Jerusalem: The Six Days That Changed the Middle East*. New York: Simon and Schuster, 1984.

Newman, David, ed. *The Impact of Gush Emunim: Politics and Settlement in the West Bank*. New York: St. Martin's Press, 1985.

Nisan, Mordechai. *Israel and the Territories: A Study in Control, 1967–1977*. Ramat Gan, Israel: Turtledove Publishing, 1978.

O'Neill, Bard E. *Armed Struggle in Palestine: A Political-Military Analysis*. Boulder, Colo.: Westview Press, 1978.

Owen, Roger. *Studies in the Economic and Social History of Palestine in the Nineteenth and Twentieth Centuries*. Carbondale: Southern Illinois University Press, 1982.

Peck, Juliana S. *The Reagan Administration and the Palestinian Question: The First Thousand Days*. Washington: Institute for Palestine Studies, 1984.

Peretz, Don. *The West Bank: History, Politics, Society and Economy*. Boulder, Colo.: Westview Press, 1986.

Peretz, Don, et al. *A Palestine Entity?* Washington: Middle East Institute, 1970.

Plascov, Avi. *The Palestinian Refugees in Jordan, 1948–1957*. London: Frank Cass, 1981.

_____. *A Palestinian State? Examining the Alternatives*. London: International Institute for Strategic Studies, 1981.

Pogany, Istvan S. *The Security Council and the Arab-Israeli-Conflict*. New York: St. Martin's Press, 1984.

Polk, William B. *The United States and the Arab World*. 3rd ed. Cambridge: Harvard University Press, 1975.

Price, David L. *Jordan and Palestinians: The PLO's Prospects*. London: Institute for the Study of Conflict, 1975.

Quandt, William. *Decade of Decisions: American Policy Toward the Arab-Israeli Conflict, 1967–1976*. Berkeley and Los Angeles: University of California Press, 1977.

Quandt, William, et al. *The Politics of Palestinian Nationalism*. Berkeley and Los Angeles: University of California Press, 1973.

Ramazani, R. K. *Beyond the Arab-Israeli Settlement*. New York: Institute of Foreign Policy Analysis, 1977.

Reich, Bernard. *Quest for Peace: United States-Israel Relations and the Arab-Israeli Conflict*. New Brunswick, N.J.: Transaction Publishers, 1977.

Richardson, John P. *The West Bank: A Portrait*. Washington: Middle East Institute, 1984.

Royal Scientific Society. *Information on Resources of the Occupied West Bank*. Amman: Royal Scientific Society, 1979.

_____. *The Significance of Some West Bank Resources to Israel*. Amman: Royal Scientific Society, 1979.

Rubenstein, Daniel. "The Jerusalem Municipality under the Ottomans, British and Jordanians." In Joel L. Kramer, ed., *Jerusalem: Problems and Prospects*. New York: Praeger, 1980.

Sahliyeh, Emile F. *In Search of Leadership: West Bank Politics Since 1967*. Washington: Brookings Institution, 1988.

_____. *The PLO After the Lebanon War*. Boulder, Colo.: Westview Press, 1986.

_____. "The West Bank Pragmatic Elite: The Uncertain Future." *Journal of Palestine Studies* 15 (Summer 1986): 34–45.

Said, Edward. *The Question of Palestine*. New York: Vintage Books, 1981.

Salem, Jamal. *The Agricultural Sector and Water Resources in the West Bank*. Amman: Royal Scientific Society, 1980. (In Arabic)

Saliba, Samir N. *The Jordan River Dispute*. The Hague: Martinus Nijoff, 1968.

Sandler, Shmuel, and Hillel Frisch. *Israel, the Palestinians, and the West Bank: A Study in Intercommunal Conflict*. Lexington, Mass.: Lexington Books, 1984.

Saunders, Harold. *The Middle East Problem in the 1980s*. Washington: American Enterprise Institute, 1981.

Scholch, Alexander, ed. *Palestinians over the Green Line: Studies on the Relations Between Palestinians on Both Sides of the 1949 Armistice Line Since 1967*. Exeter, England: Ithaca Press, 1983.

Shamir, Shimon. *Communications and Political Attitudes in West Bank Refugee Camps*. Jerusalem: Shiloah Centre for Middle East and African Studies, 1974.

Shehadeh, Raja. *Occupier's Law: Israel and the West Bank*. Washington: Institute for Palestine Studies, 1985.

_____ . *The Third Way: A Journal of Life in the West Bank: Between Mute Submission and Blind Hate*. New York: Quartet Books, 1982.

Shehadeh, Raja, and Jonathan Kuttab. *The West Bank and the Rule of Law: A Study*. Geneva: International Commission of Jurists and Law in the Service of Man, 1980.

Shemesh, Moshe. "The West Bank: Rise and Decline of Traditional Leadership, June 1967 to October 1973." *Middle Eastern Studies* 20 (July 1984): 290–323.

Shlaim, Avi. *Collusion Across the Jordan: King Abdullah, the Zionist Movement and the Partition of Palestine.* London: Oxford University Press, 1988.

Sinai, Anne, and Allen Pollack, eds. *The Hashemite Kingdom of Jordan and the West Bank: A Handbook.* New York: American Academic Association for Peace in the Middle East, 1977.

Singer, Joel. *The Establishment of a Civil Administration in the Areas Administered by Israel.* Tel Aviv: Faculty of Law, Tel Aviv University, 1982.

Smith, Pamela Ann. *Palestine and the Palestinians, 1876–1983.* New York: St. Martin's Press, 1984.

Sofer, Naim. "The Political Status of Jerusalem in the Hashemite Kingdom of Jordan, 1948–1967." *Middle Eastern Studies* 12 (January 1976): 73–94.

Spiegel, Steven L. *The Other Arab-Israeli Conflict: Making America's Middle East Policy, from Truman to Reagan.* Chicago: University of Chicago Press, 1984.

Statistical Abstract of Israel. Tel Aviv, various years.

Susser, Asher. "Jordanian Influence in the West Bank." *Jerusalem Quarterly*, no. 8 (Summer 1978): 53–65.

Sutcliffe, Claude R. "The East Ghor Canal Project: A Case Study of Refugee Resettlement, 1961–1966." *Middle East Journal* 27, no. 4 (Autumn 1973): 471–82.

Tamari, Salim. "In League with Zion: Israel's Search for a Native Pillar." *Journal of Palestine Studies* 12 (Summer 1983): 41–56.

Thorpe, Merle, Jr. *Prescription for Conflict: Israel's West Bank Settlement Policy.* Washington: Foundation for Middle East Peace, 1984.

Treatment of Palestinians in Israeli-Occupied West Bank and Gaza: Report of the National Lawyers Guild, 1977 Middle East Delegation. New York: National Lawyers Guild, 1978.

Tschirgi, Dan. *The Politics of Indecision: Origins and Implications of American Involvement with the Palestine Problem.* New York: Praeger, 1983.

Tsimhone, Daphna. "The Christian Communities in Jerusalem and the West Bank, 1948–1967." *Middle East Review* 9 (Fall 1976): 41–46.

Tuma, Elias, and Haim Darin-Drabkin. *The Economic Case for Palestine.* New York: St. Martin's Press, 1978.

Van Arkadie, Brian. *Benefits and Burdens: A Report on the West Bank and Gaza Strip Economies Since 1967.* New York: Carnegie Endowment for International Peace, 1977.

Viorst, Milton. *UNRWA and Peace in the Middle East.* Washington: Middle East Institute, 1984.

Ward, R. J., et al. *The Palestinian State: A Rational Approach.* Port Washington, N.Y.: Kennikat Press, 1977.

Wilson, Evan M. *Decision on Palestine: How the U.S. Came to Recognize Israel.* Stanford: Hoover Institution Press, 1979.

_____ . *Jerusalem: Key to Peace.* Washington: Middle East Institute, 1970.

Yost, Charles. "The Arab-Israeli War: How It Began." *Foreign Affairs* 46, no. 2 (January 1968).

JORDAN: SOCIETY AND DEVELOPMENT

Abu Hassan. *Turath al-Badu al-Qada'i* (Legacy of Bedouin Justice). Amman: Da'irat al-Thaqafa wa al-Funun, 1974.

Abu-Hilac, A. K., and I. Othman. "Jordan." In C.A.O. van Nieuwenenhuijze, ed. *Commoners, Climbers and Notables: A Sampler of Studies on Social Ranking in the Middle East.* Leiden: E. J. Brill, 1977.

Abu Jaber, Kamel. *The Jordanians and the People of Jordan.* Amman: Royal Scientific Society, 1980.

Abu Jaber, Kamel S., et al. "Socio-Economic Survey of the Badia of Northeast Jordan." Amman: University of Jordan, 1976. (Mimeographed)

Antoun, Richard T. *Arab Village: A Social Structural Study of a Transjordan Peasant Community.* Bloomington: Indiana University Press, 1972.

_____. "Conservatism and Change in the Village Community." *Human Organization* 24 (Spring 1965): 4–10.

_____. *Low-Key Politics.* Albany: State University of New York Press, 1979.

_____. "On the Modesty of Women in Arab Muslim Villages: A Study of the Accommodation of Traditions." *American Anthropologist* 22, no. 4 (August 1968): 761–97.

_____. "On the Significance of Names in an Arab Village." *Ethnology* 7 (April 1968): 158–70.

_____. "The Social Significance of Ramadan in an Arab Village." *Muslim World* 58 (January 1968): 294–308.

Aresvik, Oddvar. *The Agricultural Development of Jordan.* New York: Praeger, 1976.

Arif, Arif al-. *Al-Qada' bayn al-Badu* (Justice Among the Bedouin). Jerusalem, 1933.

_____. *Bedouin Love, Lore, and Legend.* Jerusalem: Cosmos, 1944.

Baer, G. "Land Tenure in the Hashemite Kingdom of Jordan." *Land Economics* 33 (September 1964): 622–31.

Bukhari, Najati al-. *Education in Jordan.* Amman: Ministry of Information and Culture, 1972.

Canaan, Taufiq. "Der Mord in Sitten und Gerbräuchen bei den Arabern Jordaniens." *Zeitschrift des Deutschen Palästina-Vereins,* no. 80 (1964): 85–98.

_____. "The Saqr Bedouin." *Journal of Palestine Oriental Society* 16 (1936): 21–32.

Chelhod, Joseph. *Le Droit dans la société bédouine.* Paris: Marcel Rivière, 1971.

_____. "Problèmes d'ethnologie jordanienne: Nomadisme et sédentarité." *Objets et Mondes* 7, no. 2 (Summer 1967): 85–102.

Coate, Aharon. "The Condition of Arab Refugees in Jordan." *International Affairs* 29 (October 1953): 449–56.

Copeland, Paul W. *The Land and People of Jordan.* 2nd ed. Revised by Frances Copeland Stickles. Philadelphia: J. B. Lippincott, 1972.

Cunningham, Robert B. "Dimensions of Family Loyalty in the Arab Middle East: The Case of Jordan." *Journal of Developing Areas* 8, no. 1 (October 1973): 55–64.

Dees, Joseph L. "Jordan East Ghor Canal Project." *Middle East Journal* 13, no. 4 (1955): 357–71.

Diqs, Isaak. *A Bedouin Boyhood*. London: George Allen and Unwin, 1967.

Dissard, J. "Les Migrations et les vicissitudes de la Tribu des 'Amer." *Revue Biblique*, January 18, 1905, 410–25.

Glubb, Sir John Gabot. "Economic Situation of the Transjordan Tribes." *Journal of the Royal Central Asian Society* 25 (July 1938): 448–59.

―――. *Handbook of the Nomad, Semi-nomad, Semi-sedentary and Sedentary Tribes of Syria*. GSI(T), HQ 9th Army, 1942.

Goichon, A. M. *Jordanie Réelle*. 2 vols. Paris: De Brouwer, 1967, 1972.

Graf, Erwin. *Das Rechstwesen der Heutigen Beduinen*. Beiträge zur Sprach- und Kulturgeschichte des Orients, 5. Walldorf-Hessen: Verlag für Orientkunde Dr. H. Vorndran, 1952.

Grannot, A. *The Land System in Palestine: History and Structure*. London: Eyre and Spottiswoode, 1952.

Grassmuck, George. "Regional and Local Government in the Hashemite Kingdom of Jordan." Paper delivered at the Conference on Local Government in Mediterranean Countries, American University of Beirut, September 1966.

Gubser, Peter. *Jordan: Crossroads of Middle Eastern Events.* Boulder, Colo.: Westview Press, 1983.

_____ . "Jordan: New Institutions and Processes in a Traditional Setting." In L. Cantori and I. Harik, eds., *Local Politics and Development in the Middle East.* Boulder, Colo.: Westview Press, 1983.

_____ . *Politics and Change in Al-Karak, Jordan.* Boulder, Colo.: Westview Press Encore Editions, 1985.

Hacker, James M. *Modern Amman.* Durham, England: Department of Geography, Durham Colleges, 1960.

Harris, George L. *Jordan.* New Haven, Conn.: Human Relations Area Files, 1958.

Hijazi, Nayif, and Mahmud Atallah. *Jordanian Personalities.* Amman, 1973. (In Arabic)

Jaussen, Le P. Antonin. *Coutumes des Arabes au pays de Moab.* Paris: Librairie d'Amérique et d'Orient Adrien Maisonneuve, 1948.

Jreisat, Jamil E. *Provincial Administration in Jordan: A Study of Institution Building.* Pittsburgh: University of Pittsburgh Press, 1968.

Jureidini, Paul A., and R. D. McLaurin. *Jordan: The Impact of Social Change on the Role of Tribes.* New York: Praeger, 1984.

Kazziha, Walid. *The Social History of Southern Syria (Trans-Jordan) in the Nineteenth and Early Twentieth Century.* Beirut, 1972.

Khouri, Rami G. *The Jordan Valley: Life and Society Below Sea Level.* New York: Longman, 1983.

Kilani, Faruq al-. *Al-Mahakim al-Khassa fi al-'Urdun* (Special Courts in Jordan). Beirut: Dar al-'Ilm li al-Malayin, 1966.

Lancaster, William. *The Rwala Bedouin Today*. Cambridge: Cambridge University Press, 1981.

Layne, Linda L. "Tribesmen as Citizens: 'Primordial Ties' and Democracy in Rural Jordan." In Linda L. Layne, ed., *Elections in the Middle East: Implications of Recent Trends*. Boulder, Colo.: Westview Press, 1987.

Lerner, Daniel. *The Passing of Traditional Society*. New York: Free Press, 1958.

Lewis, Norman N. *Nomads and Settlers in Syria and Jordan, 1800–1980*. New York: Cambridge University Press, 1987.

Libbey, W., and Franklin Hoskins. *The Jordan Valley and Petra*, vol. 1. New York: Putnam, 1905.

Luke, Harry, and Edward Keith-Roach. *The Handbook of Palestine and Trans-Jordan*. London: Macmillan, 1930.

Lutfiyya, A. M. *Baytin: A Jordanian Village*. The Hague: Mouton, 1966.

MacDonald, Sir Murdoch, and Partners. *Report on the Proposed Extension of Irrigation in the Jordan Valley*. London: Cook, Hammond, and Kell, 1951.

Main, Charles T. *The Unified Development of the Water Resources of the Jordan Valley Region*. Prepared at the request of the United Nations, under direction of the Tennessee Valley Authority. Boston, 1953.

Malkawi, Ahmad. *Regional Development in Jordan: Some Aspects of the Urban Bias*. Amman: Royal Scientific Society, 1978.

Mogannam, E. Theodore. "Development in the Legal System of Jordan." *Middle East Journal* 6, no. 2 (Spring 1952): 194–206.

Mostyn, Trevor, ed. *Jordan: A MEED Practical Guide*. London: Middle East Economic Digest, 1983.

Musil, A. *The Manners and Customs of the Rwala Bedouin*. New York: American Geographic Society, 1928.

Nelson, Biyar. *Azraq: Desert Oasis*. Athens: Ohio University Press, 1975.

Nyrop, Richard F., et al. *Jordan: A Country Study*. Washington: Foreign Area Studies Division, American University, 1980.

Osborn, Christine. *An Insight and Guide to Jordan*. New York: Longman, 1982.

Oweidi, Ahmad Saleh Suleiman. "Bedouin Justice in Jordan." Ph.D. dissertation, Cambridge University, 1982.

Patai, R. *The Kingdom of Jordan*. Princeton: Princeton University Press, 1958.

Peake, Frederick. *History and Tribes of Jordan*. Miami, Fla.: Miami University Press, 1958.

_____ . "Transjordan." *Journal of the Royal Central Asian Society* 26 (July 1939): 375–96.

Phillips, Paul Grounds. *The Hashemite Kingdom of Jordan: Prolegomena to a Technical Assistance Programme*. Chicago: University of Chicago Press, 1954.

Qusus, 'Awda al-. *al-Qada' al-Badawi* (Bedouin Justice). Amman: al-Matba'ah al-'Urdunniya, 1972.

Qutub, Ishaq. "The Impact of Industrialization on Social Mobility in Jordan." *Development and Change* 1, no. 12 (1969): 29–49.

_____. "Social Change in Rural Jordan: The Rise of the Middle Class." *Middle East Forum* 37, no. 10 (December 1961): 40–44.

Reese, Howard C., et al. *Area Handbook for the Hashemite Kingdom of Jordan.* Washington: U.S. Government Printing Office, 1959.

Seale, P., ed. *The Shaping of an Arab Statesman: Sharif Abd-al-Hamid and the Modern Arab World.* New York: Quartet Books, 1983.

Seton, C. R. W., ed. *Legislation of Transjordan, 1918–1930.* London: Crown Agents, [1931].

Sinai, Anne, and Allen Pollack, eds. *The Hashemite Kingdom of Jordan and the West Bank: A Handbook.* New York: American Academic Association for Peace in the Middle East, 1977.

Sutcliffe, Claud R. "The East Ghor Canal Project: A Case Study of Refugee Resettlement, 1961–66." *Middle East Journal* 27, no. 4 (Autumn 1973): 471–82.

Training Institutes in Jordan. Amman: Ministry of Information, 1978.

Weulersse, Jacques. *Paysans de Syrie et du Proche-Orient.* Paris: Gallimard, 1946.

Yorke, Valerie. "Jordan Is Not Palestine: The Demographic Factor." *Middle East International*, April 16, 1988.

Zahlan, A. B., ed. *Agriculture Sector of Jordan: Policy Systems Studies*. London, 1985.

JORDAN: ECONOMY

Abu Howayej, B. *Agricultural Atlas of Jordan*. Amman: Ministry of Agriculture, 1973.

Anani, Jawad. "Adjustment and Development: The Case of Jordan." In Daid el-Naggar, *Adjustment Policies and Development Strategies in the Arab World*. Washington: International Monetary Fund, 1987.

Aresvik, O. *The Agricultural Development of Jordan*. New York: Praeger, 1976.

Development Council. *Seven-Year Economic and Social Development Programme, 1962–1970*. Amman, Development Council, 1964.

International Bank for Reconstruction and Development. *The Economic Development of Jordan*. Baltimore: Johns Hopkins University Press, 1957.

Kanovsky, Eliyahu. *Economic Development of Jordan*. Tel Aviv: University Publishing Projects, 1977.

_____ . *The Economic Impact of the Six-Day War*. New York: Praeger, 1970.

_____ . *The Economy of Jordan: Implications of Peace in the Middle East*. Tel Aviv: University Publishing Projects, 1976.

Khader, Bichara, and Adnan Badran, eds. *The Economic Development of Jordan*. London: Croom Helm, 1987.

Konikoff, A. *Transjordan: An Economic Survey*. Jerusalem: Economic Research Institute of the Jewish Agency for Palestine, 1946.

Mazur, Michael. *Economic Growth and Development in Jordan*. Boulder, Colo.: Westview Press, 1979.

Ministry of Planning. *Five-Year Plan for Economic and Social Development, 1986–1990*. Amman, 1986.

National Planning Council. *Three-Year Development Plan, 1973–1975*. Amman, 1972.

_____. *Five-Year Plan for Economic and Social Development, 1976–1980*. Amman, 1976.

_____. *Five Year Plan for Social and Economic Development*. Amman, 1981.

Rivier, François. *Croissance industrielle dans une économie assistée: Le cas jordanien*. Beirut: Cermac, 1980.

Royal Scientific Society, Department of Economics. Occasional Publications.

Wilson, Rodney J. A. "Jordan's Trade: Past Performance and Future Prospects." *International Journal of Middle East Studies* 20 (1988): 325–44.

World Bank. *Jordan: Special Economic Report*. Washington, 1983.

Zahlan, A. B., ed. *Agriculture Sector of Jordan: Policy Systems Studies*. London, 1985.